The Finch Handbook

Christa Koepff
April Romagnano, Ph.D., DVM

With Full-color Photographs
Drawings by Gertrud Thomas

BARRON'S

All inquiries should be addressed to:
Barron's Educational Series, Inc.
250 Wireless Boulevard
Hauppauge, New York 11788
http://www.barronseduc.com

ISBN-13: 978-0-7641-1826-5
ISBN-10: 0-7641-1826-9

Library of Congress Catalog Card No. 2001025375

Library of Congress Cataloging-in-Publication Data
Koepff, Christa.
   [Neue Prachtfinken Buch. English]
   The finch handbook : purchase, care, nutrition and diseases, plus a description of more than 50 species / Christa Koepff.—2nd English ed.
      p. cm.
   Includes bibliographical references (p.).
   ISBN 0-7641-1826-9 (alk. paper)
    I. Title.
   SF473.F5 K6413   2001
   636.6′862.—dc21   2001025375

Printed in China
20 19 18 17 16 15 14

Publisher's Note
   There is some disagreement among ornithologists about the classification of some of the birds described in this book, and a variety of popular names are used for some species. The common and scientific names given for the species in this book do not in all cases agree with those given in the German original. For the English edition, the editors, with the advice of François Vuilleumier, Curator, Department of Ornithology, American Museum of Natural History, New York, have provided common names based on *Estildid Finches of the World* by Derek Goodwin (British Museum [Natural History], 1982). The Latin names are based on *Reference List of the Birds of the World* by John J. Morony, Jr., Walter J. Bock, and John Farrand, Jr. (American Museum of Natural History, New York, 1975). This treatment follows that of the *Checklist of Birds of the World*, volume XIV, edited by Raymond A. Paynter, Jr. (Museum of Comparative Zoology, Cambridge, MA, 1968), with some minor modifications based on recent research findings.

Photo Credits
   Ardea-Chapman: page 111; Ardea-Tilford: page 96; Ardea-Trounson and Clampett: pages 107, 112; Biefeld: page 131; Coleman: page 136; Coleman/Laubscher: pages 75, 76, 88; Nicolai: pages 80, 81, 84; Pforr: pages 93, 95, 123, 124; Reinhard: page 133; Scholtz: pages 69, 70, 72, 74, 78, 79, 85, 91, 92, 98, 100, 113, 117, 121, 127, 129, 130; Webb: all other photos.

Cover Photos
   B. Everett Webb

Important Note
   The subject of this book is how to take care of finches in captivity. In dealing with these birds, always remember that newly purchased birds—even when they appear perfectly healthy—may well be carriers of salmonella. This is why it is advisable to conduct a prepurchase examination and to observe strict hygienic rules. Other infectious diseases that can endanger humans, such as ornithosis and tuberculosis, are rare in passerine birds. Still, if you see a doctor because you or a member of your household has symptoms of a cold or of the flu, mention that you keep birds. No one who is allergic to feathers or feather dust should keep birds. If you have any doubts, consult your physician before you buy a bird.
   Most food insects are pests that can infest stored food and create a serious nuisance in our households. If you decide to grow any of these insects, be extremely careful to prevent them from escaping from their containers.

Contents

Preface

Certain species of finches, including waxbills, cutthroats, goldbreasts, avadavats, munias, twinspots, firefinches, and grassfinches, have long been popular pets. These species—mostly native to tropical areas of Africa, Asia, and Australia—are classified in the family Estrildidae. We refer to the varied assortment of estrildid finches as "exotic finches."

If you keep exotic finches that have lived in captivity for generations, such as Zebra Finches or Bengalese Finches, chances are that you will not run into any problems at all. Indeed, as long as you observe the basic rules of care, feeding, and breeding, your birds are likely to lay eggs, build nests, and raise young. If, however, your ambition is to have an indoor aviary with a mixed community that includes birds that have been caught wild, you should first learn all you can about them. Exotic finches come to us from a variety of different environments, and their needs and behavior are by no means uniform. Some species do not get along with others and may even attack each other ferociously.

In this book all major species of exotic finches are described in detail. In Chapter Eight, Descriptions of Exotic Finches, you will find information on the geographic origin and the natural habitat of each species, as well as hints on care and breeding.

Anyone keeping exotic finches should bear in mind that the space we offer them is never more than a poor substitute for what the birds were used to. A home for birds can therefore never be too large, and the cages and aviaries I suggest reflect the minimum requirements. I also discuss everything you need to know about acclimating exotic finches, their care, and proper diet and suggest steps you can take to help them mate and raise their young.

A detailed chapter deals with diseases and their treatment. You can save yourself a lot of trouble if you house and feed your birds properly and always keep the cage or aviary absolutely clean. Proper care—and cleanliness is an important part of care—is the best preventive measure against disease. I should like to take this opportunity

Parrot finches, like these two Pintailed finches, are spectacularly colored birds.

to thank the veterinarian April Romagnano, a specialist in avian diseases, for checking this chapter.

As an ornithologist dealing professionally with birds every day, I urge you to spend as much time as you can watching your finches. You will soon realize that many of them are real individuals. In a special chapter I explain the most important behavior patterns of exotic finches. Please read this chapter carefully because your birds' behavior can tell you a great deal about their moods and state of health. You will be able to tell whether your charges are healthy or sick, content, nervous, or aggres-

sive. In her drawings, Mrs. Gertrud Thomas has captured with great sensitivity the typical ways of these graceful and active birds. I should like to thank her as well as the photographers whose excellent color photos will familiarize you with the appearance of almost all the species mentioned.

I should like to offer my special thanks to Professor Nicolai for his patient advice in the preparation of this manuscript. This book owes much to his extensive experience in keeping exotic finches and to the research he has done on them.

Christa Koepff

Chapter One

Considerations Before You Buy

In pet shops, exotic finches often attract considerable attention. They charm people with their liveliness and pretty plumage. But before you buy a pair of these attractive birds you should be fully aware of all that is involved in taking responsibility for their lives.

Finches and Your Life

Finches are proper pets for you only if you can answer the following questions with an unqualified yes.
• Are you aware that exotic finches will never be as tame as, say, a hand-raised parakeet?
• Do you know that exotic finches must never be kept singly? They are extremely sociable birds and need partners of their own species. If they are deprived of companions, they suffer loneliness, which may manifest itself in abnormal behavior or even sickness. If you want to keep no more than one bird you should get a canary, a parakeet, or a larger parrot.
• Will you be able to arrange for appropriate care for your finches

when you are away and when they contribute to the dirt in your living quarters? Birds lose feathers, especially fine down, and they shake out dust. When they bathe, they splash water, and they scatter litter outside their cage. If you can put up with these minor annoyances without being tempted to teach the birds better manners, exotic finches will feel happy in your home.
• Because finches are so small, a novice aviculturist assumes that they will be content with a small cage. But exotic finches, more than some other birds, are very active by nature and love to move around. The full range of their charm becomes evident only if they have a chance to fly.
• Do you have enough space available for your finches so that they will not be constantly reminded of the difference between living in captivity and existing in the wild? With proper care, finches can live up to 10 or 15 years.
• Do you have enough time to care for your charges? Exotic finches need not only fresh food and water, but also some of your time and attention every day. With this in

Finches love to move around and fly.

• Are you fully aware that keeping a pair of birds is likely to result in avian offspring? Witnessing the tender affection of a bird couple is an exciting experience for a true bird lover.

• Have you perhaps set your mind on breeding several species? If that is the case and you are a beginner in the field, your first attempts should be limited to some of the easier species.

mind, can you say that birds fit your lifestyle?

• How does the rest of your family feel about your desire to keep finches? The mere fluttering about of a bird puts some people on edge, and some are allergic to the dust of feathers. Have you consulted everyone in your household?

A Group of Finches

Exotic finches are very sociable birds and should—depending on the species—be kept in pairs or larger groups. A finch that is kept singly is a lonely bird that will, in many cases, accept even a member of a different, though closely related, species to satisfy its need for companionship.

Finches are sociable birds that should be kept in pairs or larger groups.

Pet stores offer many different kinds of exotic finches for sale, and their compatibility with other birds varies from species to species. Some birds are aggressive only during the breeding period and will then attack even totally unrelated birds. You will have to keep a steady watch over your birds and remove the aggressor promptly if there are fights or chases. The weaker bird has only limited opportunity to get away from its pursuer and is often unable to eat as much food as it needs.

If you want to add one more species to your community of different finches, you can let your personal preference guide your choice. With the exception of the Crimson Finch, the Bar-breasted Firefinch, and the Common Waxbill, finches are so peaceable that they can be kept with other seed-eating songbirds. However, a few species, such as the Melba Finch, the Orange-winged Pytilia, and the Violet-eared Waxbill, are so aggressive toward closely related species that they cannot be kept together with them in an aviary. On the other hand, the Zebra Finch, the Java Sparrow, the Red-headed Parrot Finch, the Gouldian Finch, and all members of the genus *Lonchura* can be kept in flocks without any problem (see Chapter Eight, Descriptions of Exotic Finches). But be careful that neither males nor females predominate in the community because unattached birds are always on the lookout for a partner and can therefore introduce strife into the group.

Diamond Firetail finches can become aggressive toward other species at mating time.

The following list of potential bullies is organized by degree of aggressiveness, starting with species that cannot be kept together with other species and ending with those that cause trouble only occasionally.
• Crimson Finch
• Diamond Firetail
• Cutthroat
• Red-headed Finch
• Black-throated Finch
• Bar-breasted Firefinch
• Dybowski's Twinspot

Individual birds belonging to the species of potential troublemakers listed above may be perfectly

Because they are delicate and shy, finches are not ideal pets for children.

peaceful, and you may also come across aggressive individuals in species that normally do not pose problems.

People toying with the idea of raising exotic finches should ask themselves first of all whether they will have enough space for the birds. Some of the more demanding species, such as the Parrot Finches, will breed only in an indoor or outdoor aviary. If your space is limited you should therefore choose birds of a less demanding species that will raise young in a cage (such as the Bengalese Finch or Zebra Finch). If you would like to keep other kinds of birds together with your finches, you should choose ones of about the same size. Finches are afraid of birds that are much larger than they are.

They get along best with canaries, Shama Thrushes, and weavers. Many kinds of exotic birds, such as Gouldian Finches, Java Sparrows, Cordon-bleus, Lavender Waxbills, Long-tailed Grassfinches, and Zebra Finches, can usually be kept with parakeets with no problem.

Taking a Vacation

Arrange well beforehand who will look after your finches if you plan to go away on vacation. The best solution is friends or neighbors who are willing to take charge of your birds while you are gone. Make sure all the different kinds of bird food needed are on hand and give the cages and aviaries a last thorough cleaning before you leave. This will make the chore of looking after your birds while you are gone considerably easier.

The ideal solution is for another bird fancier experienced with exotic finches to step in for you during your absence. This person will know what to do even if unforeseen illness strikes or conflicts between individual birds arise. Another idea is to entrust your finches to a veterinary clinic for boarding while you are away. Consult with your avian veterinarian about these services.

Children and Finches

Generally speaking, exotic finches always keep a certain distance from people and never become as tame as a hand-raised young parakeet. Some species are characterized by shyness. Since children like to play with animals or pet them, finches are not the ideal pets for them. Many finches are so delicate that they can easily be hurt by the small hands of children. When a child is old enough to understand, parents should explain just how sensitive the birds are and how they should be treated. Show the child how much pleasure there is in merely watching these interesting birds, especially the Zebra Finches.

Finches and Other Pets

If you already have a dog or a cat and want to introduce finches into your household, you first have to get the different creatures used to each other. Even in the case of well-behaved dogs and cats, caution is in order. It is not too difficult to make a dog understand that he is to leave the birds alone. Cats are a different story, and you have to be alert to potential trouble. Never leave your cat alone with the birds because they will inevitably awaken the cat's hunting instinct. It is therefore always ill advised to let the birds fly free in a room where other pets are present.

Chapter Two

Buying Exotic Finches and Introducing Them into Your Home

Purchasing Tips

There are three ways to acquire a pair of young exotic finches:

1. You can buy the birds at a pet shop or in the pet section of a large department store.

2. You can purchase birds from a breeder.

3. You can obtain a pair from a bird fancier whose exotic finches have produced offspring.

If you decide to get your birds from a breeder you can do so with full confidence, but if the breeder did not keep the birds under proper conditions, breeding success would be unlikely. Breeders as well as pet dealers can supply you with Australian finches whose export from their native country has been forbidden by law for over 20 years.

Buying birds through the mail is a different story. If you buy from a catalog you have no way of selecting a specific bird, and you have to accept whatever is sent. The birds arrive totally bewildered by the transport and can also be injured or sick. The risk of ending up with a sick bird is simply too great to embark on this type of purchase.

When You Buy

If you decide to buy your birds from a dealer, you should first have a good look at the store. Are the birds' cages large enough? Is the food and water fresh? Do the birds get enough light and air? Are the cages clean, and is there litter on the bottom? If you see any gross inadequacies, you should try another store. After all, you want a healthy pair of birds. It is always a good idea to take someone along who knows something about these birds. The same is true if you want to buy from a breeder.

Sick and Healthy Birds

If you are not a bird expert and have to rely on your own judgment, you should pay attention to the following points:

• Is the bird you are interested in moving about the cage in a lively manner? Is it eating or drinking, preening itself, or occupied with its fellows? If a bird is sitting all fluffed

These two finches appear to be healthy.

up on a perch or on the floor of the cage with closed eyes, it is sick.

• Carefully observe the condition of the bird's plumage. Messy feathers around the cloaca are a sign of intestinal disorders often caused by insufficient cleanliness in keeping and feeding birds. Healthy birds move about and their feathers are in good condition. A sick bird is unlikely to survive even under the best of care.

• Are the legs straight and clean? The horny scales should form a smooth and even surface, and the claws should not be too long.

• If this is your first venture in bird keeping, you should pick a pair that presents no special problems in captivity. Recommended species for beginners are: Bengalese and Zebra Finches, Orange-cheeked and Swee Waxbills, Java Sparrows, African and Indian Silverbills, and Spotted, White-rumped, Chestnut, and White-headed Munias. Later, when you have more experience in keeping birds, you can always add more birds and ones of different species.

Once you have settled on a specific kind of finch, grasp the bird and remove it from the cage with a careful but secure hand. Check the feathers around the cloaca once more and ask the dealer to blow against this area of the bird's body. If the skin is red, this is a sign of dehydration, and thus illness.

The New Home

Before you go out to buy the finches of your choice you should get everything ready for them at home. Place a fully equipped cage in the spot you have planned for it, prepare the food—water should always be given fresh daily—and then go to get the new members of your household. Carry the birds home as quickly as possible in the ventilated cardboard containers that pet stores usually pack them in. Disoriented by the transport, the birds will take some time before they find their way around in their new surroundings and get used to the food. Birds that have been transported for a long time, for instance, for more than half a day, and have had no chance to feed during transport should be given food and water as soon as they reach their new home.

You should keep new birds under close observation to make sure that they are in good health.

The New Environment

Newly acquired birds should always be placed in a cage for the first few days so that you can observe their state of health. This cage should not be too small, and it should be put in a place where it can stay undisturbed day and night.
• Choose a spot that is light, free of drafts, away from stoves or radiators, and removed from activity and constant noise. The place should get enough sunlight but also include shade that the birds can retire to.
• Watch you new charges from a distance at the beginning.
• Do not make sudden movements that would only frighten your birds needlessly, and leave their surroundings unchanged until the birds are fully settled in.
• Speak to them softly at first in an even, gentle tone. Since the birds will be extremely shy at the beginning it is a good idea to drape a thin, light cloth over the cage. Paper is not suitable because its rustling alarms the birds. Once the newcomers have gotten accustomed to their cage you can gradually raise the cover.
• If the cage bottom has a grate safely separating the birds from their cage tray, then the substrate of choice, "white paper," can be covered with sand, but this is not recommended. If you must use sand, then washed builder's sand is best. Please note that, as mistakenly

believed, sand is not necessary for the digestive process of finches, is in fact dangerous, and can cause gastrointestinal impactions.

Feeding

Ask the dealer from whom you bought your birds what kind of pellets or seeds they have been eating, and mix these in with the bird food you have bought at a pet store or veterinary clinic. This helps the birds adapt quickly to the food they need to survive. Some birds will not accept unfamiliar foods readily and may starve to death with dishes full of bird food in front of them. That is why you should check after a few hours with every new bird to make sure it has found and consumed water and food.

The food and water dishes must be placed so that they are easily visible and accessible to the birds. Sometimes it helps to place some extra dishes with food and water at different heights on the walls of the cage, as well as on the grate of the cage. Dishes of food and water can be placed anywhere on the grate, as long as they are not located directly under the birds' perches.

After a few days of acclimation, introduce new soft foods and new greens only under the advice, and in the proposed time schedule, of your avian veterinarian. New kinds of food should always be given in very small amounts at the beginning. Some birds take to a new food with such a vigorous appetite that the sudden change in diet can

Food dishes for finches should be large enough to allow several birds to eat at the same time.

result in illness. Further, after their acclimation period of a few days, do not give your birds any vitamins, unless recommended by your avian veterinarian.

Medication

Never give your birds medications of any kind, unless it is with the advice and under the supervision of an avian veterinarian. Over-the-counter antibiotics given to birds, or animals of any kind, without the benefit of a professional's intervention, as well as culture and sensitivities, are always dangerous. If your bird appears off, fluffed, or lethargic, take it to your avian veterinarian immediately. All birds hide their signs of illness expertly, so once they are visible to you, the disease process is often advanced.

Sick birds: Sick birds fluff up to conserve heat. After examination and treatment, your avian veterinarian will recommend that such birds be kept warm, especially during the acclimation period. An infrared

When you introduce a new finch into an aviary, you must make sure that the other birds will accept its presence.

lamp can be used to warm these birds (see Chapter Six, Diseases).

Acclimating Birds

When you feed the birds or clean the cage you should move very cautiously and calmly in order not to frighten the birds. If they panic they flutter around so wildly that they may easily injure their wings or heads.

After 30 days, once the birds have adjusted fully to their food, you can move them to their permanent home. But do not reach into the cage to catch them. There is hardly any bird that likes to be grabbed. Instead, let them hop or fly into their new quarters and close the door slowly behind them. They will have to become familiar with new surroundings once more and learn to accept the aviary as a place that is safe and offers food. Make sure that the relocated birds find their food and water.

Introducing a New Bird

If you introduce a new bird into a community of already established ones, it will probably be chased around by them as they defend their territory. If a finch that has been living in the aviary for some time pursues the newcomer and chases it away from the food, the two birds have to be separated. If you don't want to take any chances when introducing a new finch, house it at first in a cage, which you place in the aviary, or by itself in an adjacent aviary, so that the birds can get used to each other gradually.

The exact time when you should transfer your new birds from their temporary cage to their permanent home depends entirely on the state of the birds. In case of doubt, it is better to keep them in the cage a few days longer so that you can keep an eye on them and initiate treatment if it should become necessary.

Chapter Three

Basic Rules for Housing and Care

A Good Environment

The most important decision you have to make before you bring home a bird is where you are going to house it. Of course, you will make an effort to create an environment that resembles the bird's natural habitat as much as possible.

Whether you opt for a large cage, an indoor aviary, or an outdoor aviary will depend primarily on the space you have available. For many kinds of exotic finches a cage as a full-time home is unsuitable or at least a very poor solution. To breed successfully, most finches need an indoor or outdoor aviary. If you are unable to provide an aviary but would like to have birds that mate and breed, you should restrict yourself to those species that will reproduce in a large cage.

Lighting

Regardless of whether your birds live in a cage or an aviary, you have to make sure they get sufficient light. The length of day is an important factor in the lives of exotic finches. The daylight hours have to be long enough for the birds to take in sufficient food because their rate of metabolism is very high. That is the reason birds spend so many hours of the day looking for food. During the summer the natural day is long enough, but in the winter additional light has to be provided.

In their natural habitat, exotic finches get 12 to 14 hours of bright light, and they need the same in captivity. If the source of light is not strong enough or the light hours not long enough, many finches either do not mate or are unable later to feed their young properly. If the daylight hours are prolonged too much, however, the birds do not get enough sleep. Some species, such as the Goldbreast, do not develop their full coloration if the light is not bright enough. Such birds take on a more or less dark color. If exotic finches live in a cage that is open on all sides, a normal lamp or fluorescent light is sufficient. But an overhead light is not bright enough for a box-type cage

If your finches are to remain healthy, they must have at least 12 to 14 hours of light per day.

that opens only on one side and is designed for birds that are sick or still very shy. Because of its solid walls on three sides, such a cage is too dark, and you should install a small fluorescent tube (available from dealers) on the ceiling at the front of the box. The lamps should not be too strong. For cages or aviaries that are about 40 inches (101 cm) high, 4 to 8 watts are enough; for higher structures, up to 16 watts is appropriate. Fluorescent tubes are usually white, do not flicker, and do not disturb the birds in any way.

Timers: Many bird fanciers connect the lighting to a timer so that the light goes on and off automatically at the right time. Such a timer should, if possible, be connected to a dimmer mechanism so that the lights do not go out suddenly but fade gradually over a period of a half hour. During this "falling of dusk," which is very important for

the birds, the finches seek out their resting places or nests and settle in them. If you turn the light off abruptly in the evening, brooding birds may not have time to return to their nests, and the embryos in the eggs may die or the young fledglings freeze to death. If you have to do without a dimmer mechanism, you can switch off the daytime light in the aviary in the evening and leave a weak bulb burning. This reduction in light intensity will cause the birds to retire to their sleeping places.

Heating

Quarters for exotic finches have to be equipped with a heater. These birds come from tropical regions and are used to high temperatures. This means that you have to provide the degree of warmth that the species you keep require.

Some finches sleep on branches or perches, while others sleep in nests.

Most exotic finches thrive at temperatures between 65 and 70°F (18–21°C); more delicate ones like the Gouldian Finch need 68 to 86°F (20–30°C). If you keep your birds in a living room that is heated to at least 68°F (20°C), you do not need an additional heater.

Indoor aviaries as well as the enclosed area of solidly built outdoor aviaries have to have provisions for heating. They should be heated either by the regular heating system of the house or by electric or other room heaters.

laying season; otherwise, these birds can easily catch cold or panic at the slightest nighttime disturbance.

The following list contains nest-sleeping finches that are often kept in aviaries:

Diamond Firetail	Zebra Finch
Long-tailed Grassfinch	Bronze Mannikin
	Black-and-white
Parson Finch	Mannikin
Star Finch	Magpie Mannikin
Bicheno Finch	Gray-headed
Spice Finch	Munia

Sleeping Habits

Exotic finches can be divided into nest and perch sleepers. The latter spend the night on branches or perches; the former build themselves nests. If you have nest sleepers you have to provide nesting sites and materials even if it is not egg-

A Practical Cage

Even if you are able to house your birds in an aviary, you will still need a cage. Newly purchased birds are placed in a cage for a few days of acclimation. Sick birds are separated into quarantine cages and taken immediately to the veterinarian. Sometimes, parent birds with

Stainless Steel

Stainless steel is safest for bird caging. Common and cheaper galvanized wire causes zinc toxicity. If can be made safer by spraying with vinegar to oxidize the zinc, which is scrubbed away with a brush, and then washed with warm soap and water. Brass caging is also poisonous and not recommended.

their fledglings that have just learned to fly have to be moved into a cage, as when inclement weather forbids their staying in an outdoor aviary.

In pet stores you will find a great variety of different cages, but not all of these are suitable for exotic finches. Choose one that is practical and that meets the particular needs of these birds. Cages with sloping walls, pointed roofs, or little balconies are totally unsuitable because they do not offer enough room for flying, and because the birds can

easily hurt themselves in the corners.

A cage should always be longer than it is high and offer enough room for flying. If they live in cages that are too small for them, finches lose their liveliness and get fat and lazy. You can find adequate cages at least 20 inches (50 cm) long at pet stores. Remember that a bird's home can never be too large.

The walls of open cages are made of metal bars set at ½-inch (1-cm) intervals. In a high-quality model, the cage sits on a bottom that has a removable tray. When you pull out the tray, a flap automatically covers the opening so that the birds cannot escape while you clean the cage. For access, several sliding doors that can be raised and closed again are useful. Two doors at the lower corners of the front side of the cage are useful because they allow you to reach everywhere within the cage without bothering the birds. An additional larger door in the middle facilitates the installing of nests, perches, and branches in the cage.

The best kind of cage to buy is one that is open on all sides and versatile in its uses. If you have to house an unusually timid and nervous bird in a cage for a few days, cover the cage with a light cloth so that the bird does not panic too much when there are people around. Place such a cage as near a window as possible so that the birds get plenty of sunlight.

On warm summer days you should move your birdcage onto the

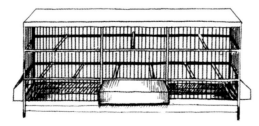

Cages can never be too large. The one shown here is suitable for a pair of exotic finches. The four walls should be made of stainless steel, and the entire cage should rest on a raised platform with a removable drawer.

Whether indoors or outdoors, an aviary should be large enough to allow resident finches to fly.

balcony where the finches can enjoy the sun. But always protect them from drafts, rain, and direct sunlight. Part of the cage should always remain in the shade.

An Indoor Aviary

In nature, birds have the whole sky as their playground, and any cage, no matter how generous, represents a severe limitation of their range of movement. As not every bird fancier has a garden where he or she can set up an outdoor aviary, the best compromise is an indoor aviary that should be large enough for the birds to fly around in. Such an indoor aviary consists of a wooden or metal frame and walls of fine wire mesh.

Size: Just how large the aviary will be depends, of course, on the size of the room that is part of, but the length, width, and height should always be in reasonable proportion to one another. Recommended dimensions for an aviary you build yourself are 80 × 40 × 60 to 80 inches (200 × 100 × 150–200 cm). Pet dealers have somewhat smaller models of about 32 × 20 × 40 inches (80 × 50 × 100 cm) for sale that are still quite adequate. Since exotic finches are expert flyers, an aviary should always be long and wide enough to allow for at least short flights. It is also desirable that the aviary be placed about 3 feet (1 m) above floor level so that you can comfortably watch your birds bathe, enjoy the sunlight, and search for food. An indoor aviary should not be placed in the middle of the room because it makes the birds nervous to be so exposed.

Placement: If you have lots of space at your disposal, you can turn a whole corner that is bright and draft free into an aviary that includes a window through which the birds can fly into a small outside area that is enclosed with wire mesh.

Equipment: You will want to equip your indoor aviary with solid perches and live branches, but make sure that there is enough open space left for flying. The best kind of branches are from willows, poplars, elderberry bushes, maples, and fruit trees.

Reeds: Some exotic finches, especially those that dwell in reeds in the wild, have claws that grow very fast. If these birds live in the wild, their claws are worn down by the reeds on which they constantly climb, and if you keep these kinds of finches inside, you will want to provide them with imitation reeds. You can do this by tying together a sheaf of reeds and leaning them in a corner of the aviary. If you are handy with tools, you may want to construct two wooden frames and stretch wire mesh over them. Mount one of them close to the bottom of the aviary and the other 12 to 16 inches (30–40 cm) above it, and stick the reeds through the mesh. You can use this same method to set up thin branches and shrubbery for nesting or attach them to the sides of the aviary.

Floor

Accessible aviary floors should be dark, textured, and washable. Pine or ash shavings and digestible paper substrates are safe.

An example of an indoor aviary where several pairs of different species can live happily. The aviary is equipped with a "bird tree," nesting boxes and baskets, various food and water dishes, and a bathing basin.

The Bird Room

If you have a very large apartment, you can give your birds a room of their own. The floor should be dark, textured, and washable, and you will want to install perches and branches but leave enough space so that the birds can move about freely. If you want to keep a fairly large flock whose members may not always get along peacefully with each other, you can use wire mesh to subdivide the room into several compartments.

A room for birds should be painted rather than papered because bacteria and fungus can easily establish themselves behind the paper. Windows should not consist of plain glass because the danger of birds flying against them is too great. Use frosted glass or glass incorporating wire mesh instead. If the windows face south, you will want to have screens for them so that the birds can benefit from fresh air and sunshine during good weather. Branches that are added to supplement artificial perches can be nailed to the wooden frames subdividing the bird room or can be screwed to the walls. You can also place potted plants such as bamboo, grape ivy, or English ivy in the corners. Branches should not stick out into the middle of the room where they can restrict the birds' flight area.

For reed-dwelling finches you can construct a reed thicket similar to that described for an indoor aviary, and if you keep Quail Finches you will want to supply a few thick tufts of grass.

Birdhouses

An ideal setup for exotic finches and one that is designed especially for serious breeders of these birds is a solidly built birdhouse with a flat roof that has several dome-shaped skylights made of plexiglass. Such a birdhouse has several rooms, each connected to a roofed-over outside area. The windows of the birdhouse should, if possible, face south so that the inner rooms get sunlight even in the winter. Rooms with windows facing north do not get direct sun at any time of year. A row of windows or glass doors separate the inside rooms from the outside areas that are protected by a projecting roof of plexiglass. It is best not to subdivide the available space into too many long but narrow aviaries, even though these would provide the opportunity to separate a number of breeding pairs that do not get along with other birds. Spaces that are nearly square are preferable because they give the finches a chance to exercise their flying skills in every direction.

Size: Suitable dimensions for the individual compartments are 9 × 12 feet (3 × 4 m) or 15 × 24 feet (5 × 8 m). If you step into an aviary of that size the birds can easily get out of your way, have less reason to panic, and will thus become quite friendly.

Your finches will be more comfortable in their home if it contains ample plants and branches.

Outside area: The outside area immediately adjacent to the wall of the building should be covered with some kind of translucent roofing material. This creates a strip about 5 feet (1.5 m) wide that is protected from precipitation and to which the birds can retire when it rains.

Landscaping: The outside aviaries of a birdhouse are landscaped with an assortment of plants that are suitable for the kinds of birds that live there. Exotic finches usually do not damage buds, and you can therefore use almost any kind of evergreen or broad-leafed tree. Choose types that have branches close to the ground, such as hedge maple, ironwood, hawthorn, dwarf birch, and common privet. The proportion of evergreen to broad-leafed trees should be about 1 to 4. Exotic

finches do not like evergreen trees to perch or sleep on, but they often seek out their branches for nesting. They also favor thick boxwoods and arborvitae as well as shrubs of the juniper family for nesting. To encourage a dense growth of branches, the trees should be pruned frequently. Exotic finches also have a special predilection for climbing around in bamboo and other kinds of reeds, and these plants usually do well in an outdoor aviary.

Other perches: In addition to the perches offered by live bushes and trees, the birds will need dowels and sturdy limbs of willow or wild cherry trees or elderberry bushes. These have to be replaced by new ones periodically. When you install perches you should make sure that they are not located directly over the water basin. If the bathing water gets contaminated with droppings, it can become the source of dangerous infectious diseases.

Water basin: The water basin, which the birds also use as a source of drinking water, is best made of natural flagstones. These should be arranged in such a way that a shallow edge is formed all around the basin. If the water is supplied by a water line and faucet, the basin can easily be cleaned at any time.

Ground covering: A good covering for the ground is pine needles over grass, which usually contains small insects that ornamental finches like to eat. Spread a fresh layer of pine needles periodically over the old, decaying ones.

Model of an outdoor aviary connected to an enclosed room to which the birds can retreat during cool weather. The left-hand third of the aviary is roofed over, and the entry on the right has a small antechamber with two doors to prevent birds from escaping.

Set up the inside rooms of the birdhouse similarly to the outside ones. Live plants will survive if sufficient amounts of light enter these rooms. The inside areas have to be large enough for your entire collection of exotic finches since the birds have to spend the major part of the year inside.

Outdoor Aviaries

In contrast to birdhouses, covered and uncovered outdoor aviaries offer a cheaper alternative for keeping exotic finches. While an uncovered outdoor aviary makes no provision for keeping out the rain, a covered one offers full protection against precipitation.

Location

The site where you locate your outside aviary should be protected from wind, drafts, and rain, and the birds have to have a bright, dry space to which they can withdraw during rainy or cold weather. It is a

Overcrowding

If you keep too many birds in an aviary, the perches and food dishes can get so dirty that weekly cleaning is not enough. More frequent cleaning means more interference with the birds. Overcrowding in an aviary has other negative consequences: Friction between birds often increases significantly because of space limitation; weaker birds find it harder to get at the food and water and disease spreads more quickly in a dirty environment. You should never keep more birds than the space you have available can comfortably accommodate.

good idea not only to cover about a third of the aviary with a tight roof, but also to surround it on all sides with walls of wood, brick, or man-made material. This creates a dry space and keeps the wind out.

The birds will still have to move to a heated room for the months from September to May in nontropical climates because there is no such thing as a winter-hardy exotic finch. Do not let any aviculturist who claims to have wintered Zebra Finches outdoors talk you into trying to do the same. Such an attempt would merely be cruel and demonstrate a lack of true concern for animals. Many species of exotic finches will not survive even one night when the temperature dips below freezing. You will find them dead the next morning.

Foundation

The foundation of an outdoor aviary has to be at least 3 feet (1 m)

It is important to place perches correctly.

deep. This is necessary because otherwise mice and rats will dig their way underneath and attack the birds in their sleep. You can place traps or poisoned bait outside the aviary, but always make sure that other animals cannot be harmed by them.

Equipment

Perches

Perches are placed in a cage in such a way that the tails of the birds will not rub against the side walls, and the perches should interfere as little as possible with the flying area. For a cage, four to five perches suffice.

Some pet stores carry spring-mounted perches that are supposed to simulate the give of natural branches. But the mechanical reaction of these perches seems to have an alarming rather than a reassuring effect on the birds and only makes them nervous.

Do not use plastic perches; use wooden ones whose surfaces can be roughened with coarse sandpaper. There is admittedly a danger that mites may lodge in the unevenness of the wood, but a rough texture is much easier for the birds to grab hold of than a smooth one. Clean and bake (200°F, 93°C) wooden perches regularly.

The thickness of the perches depends on the size of the birds' feet. For exotic finches, perches should be no thicker than ⅜ to ½ inch (1–1.2 cm). Birds that have

Common Dangers

Common dangers from which you should protect your exotic finches when they are flying free in a room are listed below.

Source of Danger	Possible Effects
Drafts caused by airing the room or by open doors and windows	Colds
Exposure to direct sunlight, overheated rooms	Heatstroke, heart attack
Sudden changes in temperature	Freezing to death, heatstroke
Glass windows or glass walls	Flying against glass, concussion, broken skull or neck
Doors	Getting caught
Open windows or doors	Flying away
Open drawers or closets	Danger of getting locked in and suffocating
Cracks between furniture and walls	Falling in the crack and getting stuck
Stoves, heaters, and electrical appliances	Getting burned
Electrical wires and outlets	Electrical shock
Candles	Getting burned
Hot pots or dishes with hot food	Burns, drowning
Kitchen vapors	Internal disorders
Traces of chemicals and cleansers	Poisoning
Open toilets	Danger of falling in and drowning
Containers full of water (pails, glasses, pots, vases)	Falling in and drowning
Empty containers	Falling in and suffocating
Knitted and crocheted items	Getting claws caught, hanging upside down
Threads and yarn	Getting head caught in a loop and strangling
Hard floors	Birds that are not yet expert flyers may land too hard and break legs or bruise chest.
Inappropriate spacing of wire or bars of cage or aviary	Getting head caught and strangling
Rusted wires, holes	Escape
Wires that are too fine and sharp	Injury to toes and head
Perches that are too small	Overgrowth of claws
Perches not fastened securely enough	Getting hit by falling perch, broken bones
Sharp objects such as ends of wire, nails, and splinters	Scratches and puncture wounds
Human feet	Getting stepped on

shrubbery in their aviaries prefer thin branches for resting and sleeping. Perches should preferably consist of soft wood. Unpeeled twigs of elderberry bushes, willows, or birches can be used but must be replaced frequently. The uneven surface of these twigs helps to keep the birds' claws worn down. Hollow bars are not suitable as perches because bird lice, mites, and other pests can establish themselves inside them.

Fastening the perch: The type of cage you have will determine how you can fasten the perches to it. For a cage consisting entirely of grating, the ends of the wooden perches may have to be whittled down somewhat. Then cut parallel notches into the ends to fit the grating and squeeze in place. For a box cage or an open one with a wooden back wall, attach the perch to the wall with a metal pin. The other end can be fastened to the grating at the front.

Floor

The outdoor aviary floor should be covered with fresh dirt and sod grass. Pine needles can be spread over the grass's regularly soiled areas. New pine needles should be periodically spread over the older decaying ones.

Dishes

Pet stores sell special china water dishes for exotic finches, but stainless steel bowls are best. These are oval in shape, measure about 6 inches (15 cm) in diameter, and about 1½ inches (4 cm) in depth. They can be used by the birds both for bathing and for drinking. Be careful not to place these dishes near any perches, or the water will get polluted with droppings.

Nesting Boxes

You should supply one to two nesting boxes per pair of finches so that the birds have some choice about where to build their nests.

Regular Care

The following list includes all the chores that are part of the regular care of exotic finches.

• *Daily:* Wash out food and water dishes with hot water and soap. Prepare fresh food. Replace water. Remove remains of food. Change birdseed. Clean floor of cage. Check temperature. Replace paper, shavings, or pine needles in the cage or aviary. Observe the birds carefully for their state of health.

• *Weekly:* Give a thorough cleaning to the cage or indoor aviary. Wash branches and perches. Clean the cage's plastic tray. Rake the soil in an outdoor aviary. Wash flagstones.

• *Monthly:* Thoroughly clean the ground of an outdoor aviary. Check the aviary for holes. Change branches and twigs. Examine the birds for parasites living on their outer surfaces. Clean out nesting and sleeping boxes. As soon as fledglings have learned to fly and no longer return to their parents' nest to sleep, the nesting box should be cleaned out thoroughly.

You should settle on a certain day of the week when you always do the weekly chores for your birds.

Feeding Time

Feedings should also take place at a set time, preferably early in the morning. Fresh fruits and vegetables spoil quickly and should be removed from the cage in the afternoon. Adhere to the feeding times even on weekends, especially for parent birds that feed their young. If you delay the feedings even a few hours, some of the more sensitive birds may no longer be able to feed their fledglings.

Nestlings

If your finches are sitting on eggs or have nestlings, you should clean the cage quickly and with great caution so that the birds will not abandon their nests prematurely. With particularly sensitive birds you should postpone all cleaning chores till later and do nothing more than change the water and give food.

Important note: It is best to use hot water and mild soap for washing cages and all objects birds need, especially food bowls; however, these items should be rinsed very thoroughly.

Escape Is Deadly

Exotic finches find many ways of escaping: doors and windows that have been left open, gates of cages or aviaries that have not been shut properly, or deteriorating wire mesh

If your finch escapes from its cage or aviary, it could suffer serious injury. Always supervise your bird carefully if you allow it outside of the cage or aviary.

that allows them to slip through. As a rule, exotic finches that find their way to freedom die very soon because they cannot find enough food or because the nights are too cold for them.

Accidents, sometimes fatal, can befall exotic finches even in a closed room. If you give your birds an occasional opportunity to fly free, you have to make sure that the windows do not look like clear openings to the outside. The best way to accomplish this is to draw the curtains. If a bird bumps against the glass of a window it may break its neck. In my opinion, free flying in a room is too fraught with danger for exotic finches; they get hurt or perish too often.

Chapter Four

Feeding Exotic Finches

Feeding Birds

Almost all the kinds of food you can offer exotic finches in captivity are substitutes for what these birds would eat in the wild, and the finches first have to get used to them.

To minimize the danger of nutritional deficiencies and intestinal problems, you should try to offer as varied a diet as possible. Perishable foods such as fruits, vegetables, and insects must always be absolutely fresh. Place the food dishes at a good distance from the water basin, because food that has water splashed on it spoils more easily. Never put food directly under the perches or it will be contaminated by droppings, the most common source of infections.

Finches eat an amount of food equivalent to one third of their body weight daily, hence, nutrients are used up very rapidly in their digestive tracts, so rapidly, in fact, that a finch can starve to death within 36 hours; therefore, regular and scheduled feedings are of paramount importance to finches. Otherwise, they are naturally very hardy birds and should live up to 15 years in captivity; unfortunately, they typically die around three years of age due to poor, unbalanced seed diet supplemented with homemade moist concoctions.

Basic Food

Most wild exotic finches feed primarily on grass seeds, but in captivity they easily adapt to various kinds of millet and canary seeds. If born in captivity, pelleted diets are best because a finch's basic diet is made up of small-grained and large-grained millets, along with canary seeds. The small-grained millets are essential for all exotic finches, and larger species like the waxbills also like large-grained millet.

Commercially Prepared Diets

The best way to feed your finch properly is to rely on commercially prepared diets. It is highly recommended that you choose to feed commercial pelleted diets over the various commercially available seed mixes. Two American companies that have excellent finch pellet and seed mixture products are Lafebers Co. and Kaytee Products, Inc.

Conversion

If you purchase a finch from a knowledgeable aviculturist who weaned your bird onto pellets, by all means continue this excellent diet choice. However, if your bird comes to you a seedeater, or "seed junkie," the conversion to a pelleted diet is an arduous process that should be supervised by your avian veterinarian. Conversion from a seed diet to a pellet diet is difficult in most psittacine and passerine birds, but it is particularly dangerous in small passerines such as finches; therefore, it is best that you seek the expertise and advice of your avian veterinarian for, as previously mentioned, finches can indeed starve to death within 36 hours. Many birds, not just finches, will choose to starve rather then eat a food they do not like or recognize. Although supervised conversion is a chore, it can be done, and should be attempted, especially since we know that the principal cause of premature death at approximately age three in the majority of captive finches is malnutrition. This malnutrition results from seed diets that are very high in fat, low in vitamins and minerals, especially vitamin A, and contain imbalanced proteins.

If your conversion is a success, and your bird is eating a pelleted diet as its base diet, then you can choose to offer the various commercial seed mixes (or Lafeber Nutri-

Finches can eat a variety of foods.

Berries or Avi-Cakes) and the occasional insect as treat items. However, if you choose to do this, only offer these items after your bird has eaten its base diet for the day; therefore, later in the day is best. Fresh fruits and vegetables, on the other hand, should make up 15 percent of your bird's diet, regardless of the base diet choice, and should be offered daily in the morning but removed in the afternoon.

If you do not succeed in your conversion attempt, and your bird continues to be a "seed junkie," then in addition to its morning commercial seed mix and fresh fruits and vegetables, you should offer either Lafeber Nutri-Berries or Avi-Cakes and the occasional insect as a treat. The Lafeber products are made from a mixture of the following: various types of prehulled, human-grade millet; other seeds and grains mixed with molasses; eggs; essential amino acids; vitamins, especially vitamin A;

and minerals. They are very palatable and highly nutritious products. Further, up to 96 percent of these Lafeber products are typically eaten, resulting in little waste, and therefore minimal mess. If your bird prefers these products to seed mixes, it is a good idea to offer them solely as the base diet, again supplemented with 15 percent fresh fruits and vegetables early in the day.

You can purchase pelleted diets, commercial seed mixes, or Lafeber Nutri-Berries or Avi-Cakes from your local pet store or avian veterinarian. Be sure to purchase only securely packaged products that are properly sealed, and always check the package dates. Never buy seed or seed products from a storage bin or other such container. Such sources are likely to be contaminated with roaches, ants, bacteria, or fungus, and may possibly be routinely snacked on by resident rodents. Further, improperly kept seed is less likely to be fresh and may become rancid. Old seed is especially dangerous if kept damp, as it may grow aflatoxins, fungal organisms, or bacterial organisms, which could kill your bird.

Fresh Fruits and Vegetables

There are many fresh fruits and vegetables preferred by finches, especially good-sized pieces of kale or romaine lettuce; apples and oranges suspended in the birds' cage by a food clip or holder are particularly attractive to them. Fresh chopped fruits and vegetables are also nutritious and appealing, and should be offered daily in their own dish.

Mealworms

A popular insect treat for pet finches is mealworms, the larval form of the darkling beetle, but birds will only rarely eat live mealworms, even when they are quite small. They prefer chopped and freshly scalded or just hatched mealworms, and they do not eat the entire larva

Mealworms make a nice treat for finches.

Raising mealworms at home is not difficult.

but suck out only the inside and leave the empty chitin shell. Mealworms can be purchased at pet stores or from other bird fanciers who raise them for their own birds.

Generally, mealworms are kept in one or two wooden boxes 12 to 16 inches (30–40 cm) long and 8 inches (20 cm) high with a cover that has air holes. Fill half full with bran, add some mealworms, and cover with a cloth. Feed the mealworms by placing slices of turnip, lettuce leaves, and stale bread on top of the bran.

If you want to raise mealworms for your birds, you will want to have several boxes like the ones described above for mealworms at different stages of development. Let some of the larvae pupate. From the pupae, black darkling beetles whose eggs will turn into more mealworm larvae will hatch. As soon as the mealworms are large enough, collect them and feed them to the birds. When the supply of one box is exhausted, fill the box again with new bran, fresh food, and young beetles.

The mealworm boxes should be kept in a warm, dark place. If the temperature is too low, the life cycle of the beetles is slowed down.

Insect Treats

Daphnia, fruitflies, enchytraeids (segmented worms like earthworms), and waxmoth larvae—all of which are sometimes found at pet stores—can be used as treats in the diet of exotic finches. These live foods are particularly helpful in the raising of young birds. If you like, you can collect daphnia yourself from small, clean puddles of water.

You can raise the larvae of the greater waxmoth yourself, too, but this is considerably more difficult than producing mealworms. The larvae of the waxmoth live inside beehives and feed on the old skins of bee larvae. Get old, no longer usable frames with some adult waxmoths from a beekeeper and keep the honeycomb in jars in a cool place. Two weeks before you plan to feed your birds waxmoths, bring a section of honeycomb into the warm house, and the deposited eggs will develop into larvae. Place the honeycomb into the aviary as a treat and the birds will pick out the insects.

The many small insects in their various developmental stages living on meadow plants in temperate climates are also a favorite food of birds and are particularly helpful during the rearing season. You can gather these minute creatures by running a butterfly net over meadow plants.

Ant pupae are another important source of animal protein. You can collect the pupae of small meadow ants from underneath stones and rotting pieces of wood and keep them for a few days in the refrigerator in jars with some earth in them. If you have large amounts, you can freeze them.

Ant pupae: The purpae of the small meadow ants make a more suitable food for raising young birds than those of larger red ants. Take care when collecting and feeding ant pupae, especially in the South.

Finches like to eat the seeds of a variety of plants.

Avoid small red ants called fire ants altogether, as this species can kill finches of all ages with their painful skin-necrotizing toxic bites. You can place the fresh pupae in the freezer for as long as you like, but let them thaw to room temperature before feeding them to the birds.

Pet stores also have dried ant pupae for sale, and many bird fanciers recommend these dried pupae, but my experience has been that most exotic finches refuse to eat the pupae, even if they have been moistened with milk or soaked in water and mixed in with other kinds of food.

Greens

The seeds of a number of grasses and other plants are the best substitute for ripening seeds, which form the basis of many exotic finches' diet for a good part of the year in their native habitat. Some favorite seeds are those of annual paniculate grasses, chickweed, common groundsel, dandelion, sow thistle, knotweed, lady's thumb, shepherd's purse, English rye grass, and wild millets. Give the birds the entire seed head with the stem, except in the case of dandelions. With these, pick off just the top after all the yellow petals have fallen off. With chickweed, feed the entire plant because the birds not only eat the seeds but also pick at the leaves. You can find fresh greens in meadows and fields and along country lanes in temperate climates. Avoid picking them along roads, because plants growing there are contaminated with exhaust fumes.

Homegrown millet is very popular with exotic finches. Harvest the ears of seed in the fall when they are partially ripe. If you have a large garden or a field, plant a good-size plot of millet, but be sure to protect it against sparrows and other birds as the seed starts to mature.

Vitamins and Minerals

If your exotic finches eat a commercial pelleted diet, then supplementing it with vitamins could cause dangerous overdoses. However, if your birds are on a predominately seed diet, then vitamin supplements are necessary, but they should be supervised by your avian veterinarian. Various brands of bird vitamins and minerals are available, and should be purchased directly from your avian veterinarian, or under his or her supervision. Most birds will refuse to drink water that is discolored or that tastes strongly of vitamins; therefore, a second, fresh, unmedicated water bowl should always be available when first introducing a new vitamin-water mix, or your birds may stop drinking altogether and die.

Calcium

Hens should always have a safe source of calcium available, especially if they are not on a pelleted diet. When breeding, finches, regardless of diet, should have access to a calcium source. The safest source is the cuttlebone of the cuttlefish. Purchase cuttlebone whole, and offer it suspended in the bird's cage, with the soft side toward the bird, for ease of nibbling. It can also be offered crushed or crumbled, and served sprinkled over the bird's diet.

Chicken eggshells are not a safe source of calcium, as the risk of infection from salmonella and other microbial agents is too great, especially when offered raw. Further, in general, eggs, high in cholesterol, are a poor protein food source for birds, which are predisposed to arthrosclerosis.

Water

Water for both drinking and bathing should be offered to exotic finches in shallow basins. Fresh, clean water has to be given every morning. The birds will immediately make use of any opportunity to splash in water. Since they fail to distinguish between drinking and bathing water, special drinking dishes, which they will hardly pay attention to, are superfluous. During hot summer weather, the water should be changed several times a day. The best kind of water containers are oval plastic dishes available at pet stores that can be filled with water up to a depth of about 1 inch (2–3 cm).

Chapter Five

Mating Your Birds and Raising the Young

First Considerations

Raising exotic finches is the common ambition of most fanciers beyond the beginner's stage, but it does require experience with birds. If you are going to raise young birds, you have to be able to house them adequately and look after them properly. You should therefore seriously ask yourself before you mate your birds whether you are prepared to take on the responsibility of having young birds. If the birds are healthy and if they do in fact mate after the courtship ritual, you can look forward to four to six hatchlings. Will you want to keep them all or will you be able to find homes for some of them? Assuming that you have sufficient space at your disposal, you still have to ask yourself whether you are prepared to spend the extra time and money the increase in your flock will demand.

Living Conditions

Impeccable living conditions are the prime factor in raising healthy young birds. Many a fancier of exotic finches has a healthy pair of birds with splendid plumage, but they refuse to breed. This may be because different species of exotic finches have very different requirements for housing, food, and nesting sites. Some birds will mate even in a flight cage, while others require a large, densely planted aviary. For some birds you have to add more protection to their cage or aviary; others need to be moved to a different aviary before you get positive results. In some cases too one-sided a diet may be the reason why the birds refuse to enter the mating phase. Switch to different kinds of fresh fruit and vegetables periodically in an effort to imitate the wide variety of food sources available in the birds' natural habitat. It is not easy to figure out just what the specific requirements of a particular pair of birds are, but it is well worth your efforts to try.

Health of the Birds

One important prerequisite for successful breeding is that the birds be strong and that they not be constantly chased by other members of the aviary community. Birds that are picked on by others never attempt to breed.

Newly imported exotic finches—no matter how healthy—need several months to adjust to the drastic changes in length of day, temperature, and type of food.

Pair Formation

In some types of exotic finches, the coloration of the male and the female is the same. This makes it very difficult to pair the birds. Some keepers of exotic finches keep a flock of mixed birds in one aviary but mark the males and females with differently colored rings. First, pairs of males and females will form, then, if several birds of the same sex are left over, these may pair off.

Exotic finches are often very fussy about choosing a partner and will mate only with a partner they really like. If at all possible, you should therefore keep exotic finches in a community so that the birds have a chance to pick a mate of their liking. Just how the courtship proceeds is described in Chapter Seven, Understanding Exotic Finches.

Most exotic finches should be at least nine to ten months old before they mate; this is the age at which they reach sexual maturity. Some species, such as the Zebra Finch, that come from arid regions are fully mature at three months; this is a result of adaptation to environmental conditions that impose early maturity for successful raising of the young. However, even with these species, it is better to delay the first

For finches to mate, they need to be housed under the proper conditions.

mating for two or three months past the time when sexual maturity is gained.

If you buy birds that already have adult plumage, you should wait about six months before providing nesting sites because you will not be able to ascertain their exact age.

Finches are fussy about mating, so you may have to give them some choice of partners.

Building a Nest

Size

Most exotic finches like to build their nests in the dense growth of bushes such as hawthorn or privet or in branches of pine or gorse attached to the wall of the aviary. However, many will accept artificial nesting sites. Nesting boxes, available for a few dollars at pet stores, should not be too small: They should be about 5½ inches (14 cm) long, a little under 4½ inches (11 cm) wide, and a little over 4½ inches (11 cm) high.

Types of Nesting Boxes

Enclosed nesting boxes have a removable top to allow the keeper to check on the nest, and their only opening is a U-shaped entry hole. Parrot Finches readily accept this kind of nesting box.

In half-open nesting boxes, the upper half of the front is open. Pytilias, Twinspots, and most waxbills prefer this kind of nesting box to the closed ones. Violet-eared Waxbills and Purple Grenadiers generally refuse to nest in boxes and build their nests instead in thick boxwood or arborvitae branches.

Placement

If you have made up your mind that you want to raise exotic finches, you should place all the nesting boxes you have in different parts of the aviary or hang them in the cage. Do not place the boxes too high, or you will be unable to watch comfortably the proceedings that are about to follow.

Building Material

Once a pair has settled on a box or a nesting site in the bushes—figure on one to two sites per pair—the male will go off in search of building material. In captivity, exotic finches will accept building materials that they would not find in nature as long as these resemble the materials the birds would naturally use. For most kinds of exotic finches, coconut fiber, available at pet stores, should be offered as the basic building material, and many birds also accept the dry leaves and inflorescenes of various grasses. Parrot Finches favor broad-leafed grasses and reeds. Other useful materials for nest building are moss, soft hay, dog hair, and sisal fiber taken from cords that are cut into 4-inch (10-cm) lengths. Agave fiber and oakum, on the other hand, are not usable and are even dangerous because these fibers get wrapped around the birds' feet easily, cut off blood circulation, and can thus lead to the loss of a leg. The tangled up balls of coconut fiber one sometimes sees for sale

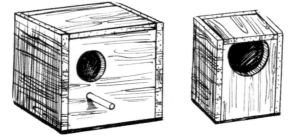

Enclosed nesting boxes with removable covers for nest checks.

are also unusable because the birds get caught in the knots and loops. Supply a wide range of nesting materials and let the birds make their own choice.

Both partners work together in the building of the nest. The male brings the materials, and the female incorporates them into the nest. Most exotic finches build their nests in the shape of spheres or baking ovens. Some kinds, such as the Black-cheeked Waxbill, expand the entry into the nest into a regular passageway.

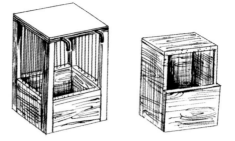

Some species of finches prefer semi-open boxes for nesting.

Egg Laying and Incubation

Most exotic finches lay four to six white eggs at daily intervals. After the third or fourth egg, the female usually begins to sit, although the pair starts spending the night in the nest beforehand. They also spend part of the day in the nest. During the day, the parents alternate sitting on the eggs about every hour and a half. During the night, it is always the female that sits on the eggs, although in many species both birds sleep in the nest.

Incubation and the rearing of newly hatched birds works out best if the birds are bothered as little as possible. Avoid all interference, especially while the birds are sitting on their eggs, but you should still keep regular watch so that you can step in if something unforeseen,

such as disturbance by other mating birds, threatens to disrupt the normal course of events.

Beginners in the art of breeding exotic finches should, if at all possible, avoid checking the nests. Some birds react very negatively to such checks, while others that have been bred in captivity for generations will put up with your occasional glance into the nest. Birds of this latter kind may even let you move their nesting box.

If you do not want your birds to produce offspring, you will have to remove the eggs and replace them with fake ones of appropriate size and color (available at pet stores).

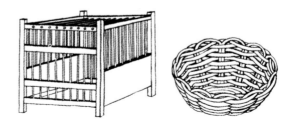

A Harz box and, on the right, a rattan basket that can be placed inside a nesting box.

Hatching and Rearing

Nesting food: The incubation period of different kinds of exotic finches varies between 11 and 14 days. As nesting feed for the following weeks, the parent birds will need a large assortment of different foods such as ant pupae, egg food, waxmoth larvae, daphnia, enchytraeids, mealworms, small insects, immature seeds of grass and other plants, and chickweed. This is also the time when the birds need more calcium and other minerals than usual.

Newly hatched birds beg for food by raising their heads diagonally to the front. Later on, they will—with the exception of the Cutthroat—lie down prone and only raise up their opened beaks.

Colors: The skin of the nestlings is flesh colored at first and becomes dark later. In most species, it is covered with white or gray down. Between the sixth and eighth day after hatching, the first signs of down feathers will appear, and these feathers will break open from the tenth day on. The eyes open on the sixth day.

Sitting on the young: Most exotic finches sit and warm the hatchlings day and night by keeping them under their wings for the first ten days. After that they sit on them only at night. Pintailed Parrot Finches sit on their young day and night for only eight days and protect them at night for only two more days. The tenth day often ushers in a critical period: The parent birds may start neglecting their perfectly normal fledglings or leave them altogether. This behavior does not spring from any lack of "parental love" but simply marks the onset of a new urge to build a nest and mate, an urge that supersedes and inhibits the instinct to feed the young. In an aviary, the birds are not occupied all day with the search for food, and the male often starts once more to court the female and lure her to a new nesting site. If this happens, catch the male and house him far enough away that the female can no longer hear him. In most cases, the female will then focus her attention on her young once again and resume feeding them.

A male Violet-eared Waxbill feeding a young bird that has already left the nest.

Moving the cage: If both parents start neglecting their young, move the whole family, nest and all, to a cage. Place the cage in a quiet room and drape a light cloth over it. However, this method works only if the hatchlings are far enough developed to have some feathers, because the parent birds will no longer sit on them if they are in unfamiliar surroundings. If the young birds have not grown any feathers yet, all you can do is remove one of the parent birds.

Splitting up the family: If these difficulties arise after the young birds have learned to fly, split up the family. House the father and the mother in separate cages, each with some of the offspring. There cannot be any contact between the two parent birds. If one of them refuses to feed the young in his or her cage, these are moved into the cage of the other parent, and the uncooperative partner is kept separated from the rest of the family until the young can take care of themselves.

Leaving the nest: The young of most exotic finches leave the nest at about three weeks, and you have to prepare new quarters for them before this happens. Jameson's Firefinches and Lavender Waxbills spend the shortest time in the parental nest (17 and 16 to 18 days, respectively), and Java Sparrows the longest (21 to 28 days). Since birds that are learning to fly are quite awkward, their first flying efforts often end with a collision against a wall or a landing in a water basin where the young birds can easily drown. Make sure, therefore, that any deep water basins are empty at this time, and offer drinking water in very shallow dishes. Keep the young birds inside in the evening and during bad weather because they become ill easily at this stage.

One further rule for raising exotic finches: All birds of this kind should raise young no more than two to three times a year. Otherwise, the females may become hypocalcemic and develop osteoporosis, which could lead to pathologic fractures and death. Prevent additional matings by removing all nesting sites.

Chapter Six

Diseases

External Signs

You can easily spot an exotic finch that is not feeling well by its listless behavior. It will hardly move, will avoid other birds, and will sit on a branch without taking any interest in anything, head facing back. Signs of ill health are fluffed-up feathers, only partially opened eyes, and irregular, labored breathing. If the bird is very sick, it will no longer sit upright on its perch but will assume a horizontal position with the tail drooping slightly downward, or it will squat weakly on the floor.

Initial Measures

If one of your birds looks sick, call your avian veterinarian and immediately have the bird seen. *Do not wait.* Finches need immediate medical care because, as with all birds, they expertly mask their illness, and by the time you note a problem, the bird is quite ill. If, after hospital treatment, your veterinarian recommends further treatment at home, keep the sick bird separated for the entire treatment and recovery period. Put it

in a smaller "quarantine" cage (see below) that is kept in a warmer, quiet area with minimal disturbances. Warmth can be safely provided by using a heat or infrared lamp at a safe distance from the bird's cage. In cases of salmonellosis or coccidiosis, you also minimize the danger of other birds getting infected.

If a bird has some internal disorder diagnosed by your avian veterinarian, supplement the usual diet with some easily digestible food such as ant pupae, finely chopped mealworms, or small insects (if acceptable to your veterinarian).

Quarantine Cages

The best kind of quarantine cage is a box cage about 40 × 12 × 16 inches (100 × 30 × 40 cm) or 30 × 14 × 17 inches (75 × 35 × 43 cm) that has grating at the front, and a removable bottom tray. Lining the tray with white paper on newspaper helps you keep daily track of the digestion of your patient. A normal bird has three parts to its droppings: the green fecal portion, the white urate portion, and the clear liquid urine portion. If the feces change color, check the food tray and compare the shades. If the feces become loose, if the urates become yellowish, or if excess urine appears to be produced, call your avian veterinarian immediately.

For aviculturists with a knack for building things, pet stores have kits for bird boxes that can serve as quarantine cages.

Temperature

Install several perches in the quarantine cage and place a 100- or 150-watt infrared light about 2 inches (5 cm) away from the front of the cage so that the sick bird is bathed in the light when it sits on the foremost perch only. This will give it the opportunity to bask close to the heat lamp or to retreat to perches farther back, where it is cooler. At first it will spend all its time close to the lamp with fluffed-up feathers to absorb the heat, but as it gets better it will gradually move farther away.

If you use a stronger infrared bulb (250 watt), the distance between lamp and cage should be about 16 inches (40 cm), or the temperature inside the cage will rise too much.

The temperature in the back of the cage should never rise above the normal indoor temperature of 68 to 72°F (20–22°C); otherwise, the bird will suffer from the excessive heat. It is important to check the temperature in the cage several times a day. Cages with four solid walls should not be used because birds can die of heatstroke in them. Nor should you use a heater that is not a lamp. At night, the infrared light helps birds find their way around the cage, feed, and move to the right warmth. Brief exposure to a heat lamp is useless. Place food and water in the cooler part of the cage to keep it from getting warm and spoiling.

A sick bird should be placed in a quarantine cage, and moved away from other birds.

Separate the Birds

If you keep the quarantine cage in the same room with the other birds, the patient will want to join them and will keep calling, which will considerably weaken it. Move the quarantine cage to a completely separate room and leave the patient in the sickroom quarters for a few days after it has recovered so that you can check on its progress.

Medicine Cabinet for Birds

Aviculturists should have supplies for first aid on hand, but should always call their avian veterinarian first. A medicine cabinet for birds should include the following items:
• a heat lamp with an infrared bulb of 100 or 150 watts,
• several pairs of tweezers, both blunt and pointed,
• Q-tips,
• a pair of small scissors,
• Band-Aids,

A clear sign of illness: The bird squats on the floor of the cage, its feathers fluffed up and its eyes closed.

• Quick-Stop,
• Betadine Scrub,
• alcohol,
• a disinfectant for cleaning cages.

Common Disorders

Colds

Symptoms: The bird sits around listlessly with fluffed-up feathers and sleeps a lot. Also, the bird has diarrhea.

Cause: If environmental factors such as drafts, dampness, or an excessive drop in temperature have weakened a bird's general resistance, germs can rapidly multiply and cause sickness.

Treatment: Call your avian veterinarian, then move the bird to a quarantine cage with an infrared lamp as quickly as possible. Next, bring the bird to your avian veterinarian in the quarantine cage. After your bird is seen and treated at the veterinary hospital, you may need to continue medications at home, as long as the bird is still eating. If the bird stops eating, then it needs to be left at the veterinary hospital to be tube fed. Once the bird begins eating again, treatment can continue at home. Be very careful when treating sick finches. For oral medications, prepare your syringe or dropper. When all is ready, and all doors are closed, hold the bird carefully but firmly in your nondominant hand. Put the medicine carefully into the bird's beak by sieve action, beginning at the commissure of the bird's beak. Once it is treated, immediately put the bird down in its cage. If you hold it longer than necessary, it might suffocate because a defense mechanism might cause the liquid to go down the trachea and into the lungs. Antibiotics are always given for a period of five days.

Intestinal Disorders

The intestinal disorders that most commonly affect exotic finches are salmonellosis and coccidiosis.

Symptoms: The bird sits around listlessly with fluffed-up feathers and sleeps a lot. The lower abdomen is red and swollen.

Cause: Inappropriate or contaminated food or dirty drinking water. Intestinal problems are almost always the result of "catching cold." Colds and intestinal disorders usually occur together and constitute the most common health problem of small birds.

Treatment: Isolate the sick bird immediately in a separate cage, supplying warmth with an infrared lamp. Call your avian veterinarian. Birds with intestinal disorders should undergo blood work and cloacal culture and sensitivity. Appropriate antibiotic therapy must be combined with good hygiene.

Salmonellosis

Symptoms: Clinical signs include diarrhea, fluffed plumage, and lethargy.

Cause: Salmonellosis is caused by bacteria of the genus *Salmonella*, and the disease is commonly introduced into an aviary by a recently acquired, infected bird. (That is why all new birds belong in quarantine for a minimum of 30 days.)

The diagnosis of salmonella is confirmed after culture and identification of the microorganism. Further, dead birds, as always, should undergo a complete necropsy and histopathology to corroborate or make the diagnosis.

Treatment: Your avian veterinarian will be able to choose the best course of treatment based on culture and sensitivities, as well as blood work. Fluids are an integral part of any intestinal disorder treatment. A month later, therapy cultures should be rescreened. Treatment and hygienic measures are repeated until cultures are negative.

Coccidiosis

Symptoms: Clinical signs include diarrhea and emaciation. Affected birds are fluffed and lethargic.

Cause: Coccidiosis is caused by the protozoan parasite that lives within the intestinal wall. At necropsy, the upper small intestine is edematous and hemorrhagic. Scrapings of this tissue reveal the parasite. Wet preparations of bird droppings help your avian veterinarian identify the parasite easily before the bird's death.

Treatment: After exact diagnosis by your avian veterinarian, treatment is likely to incorporate the recommendation of strict hygiene as well as coccidiostatic drugs. Treatment can last for as long as three weeks and is followed up by retesting of the affected birds. Be sure your birds drink well and remain hydrated throughout their treatment. Before each treatment course, the birds' cage/environment needs to be thoroughly cleaned. Flight cages or outdoor aviaries are particularly difficult to disinfect. These areas should be stripped of all greenery, wood, wood perches, nests, nesting material, and dirt. Metal surfaces need to be scrubbed down and thoroughly disinfected, as do food bowls and disinfectable toys not made out of wood or other natural materials.

Eye Infections

Symptoms: Clinical signs include swollen or sticky eyelids or conjunctiva. Birds tear excessively and may exhibit squinting.

Cause: Inflammation of the eyelids and conjunctiva can be caused by external factors, such as foreign bodies, or can be infectious. Your avian veterinarian will culture and stain the eyes to check for microbial organisms and corneal ulcers, respectively.

Treatment: If infectious, ophthalmic antibiotic drops or ointment are prescribed. If the bird has an ulcer, follow-up examinations are necessary. Foreign bodies can be dislodged and flushed away with sterile saline eyewash.

Fractures

Symptoms: Dragging wing or total inability to fly, favoring of the injured leg when perched or walking, or leg that hangs down uselessly.

Cause: Fractures occur when birds crash against windows or fly around wildly in the dark. To avoid the first danger, use glass incorporating wire mesh in the aviary instead of regular window glass; to prevent frenzied flying in the evening, avoid switching the light off suddenly and give the birds enough time to retire to their sleeping places calmly.

Treatment: Isolate the injured bird and leave it as undisturbed as possible, then call your avian veterinarian. Splints or external function devices should be applied only by a veterinarian because improper handling of these small, delicate birds by laypersons tends to aggravate rather than help the problem. Also, the bird will keep trying to get rid of a poorly attached bandage, not only tiring itself needlessly but also disturbing the bandage. Broken bones typically heal within a few weeks. During this time, the affected bird should be kept alone in a quarantine cage without a perch. Food and water bowls should be shallow bowls on the papered cage bottom.

Egg Binding

Symptoms: A female affected with this ailment sits in front of her nest or on the floor of the aviary with raised feathers and keeps trying to push. If she does not succeed in passing the fully formed egg, she will die rather quickly.

Cause: The primary cause of egg binding is hypocalcemia resulting from an all-seed diet. Also, a first-time layer, an egg that is too big, or a lack of exercise in a small cage can cause egg binding.

Treatment: Move the female immediately to a cage with an infrared lamp and call your avian veterinarian. Do not try to remove the egg. This is much too dangerous and should be attempted only by an experienced veterinarian. To save the bird, bring it to the veterinarian immediately, as intervention must occur within the first hours of straining.

Egg binding can usually be prevented if the bird is on a pelleted or well-supplemented commercial seed diet.

Rickets and Osteomalacia

Symptoms: The symptoms of these diseases are deformed feet, toes, or wings. The bones are rubbery and soft because they are deficient in calcium.

Cause: Rickets and osteomalacia occur because of specific deficiencies in vitamin D3, calcium, and phosphorus.

Treatment: Once rickets or osteomalacia is present, there is no cure; therefore, the best defense is a proper diet for the parents, especially during the rearing of the young. Pelleted diets are best, but commercial seed mixes, properly supplemented, can also be adequate.

Staggers

Symptoms: At first, the weakened bird simply rests on the stomach—as birds do in the course of many illnesses—but the head and beak are raised high. Later the bird is no longer able to land accurately on branches and perches but tumbles to the ground instead, staggers around, and ultimately dies while in convulsion.

Cause: This dreaded disease results from vitamin B and vitamin E deficiencies. By mixing rancid cod liver oil or mixing oil through the seed, encephalomalacia and fertility problems are seen because of the resulting vitamin E deficiencies. Vitamin B deficiency can cause CNS disturbances, as well as reduced hatching, stunting, and molting problems. Gouldian Finches are particularly affected.

Treatment: If you catch the disease in its earliest stages you can cure your birds quickly by adding vitamins to the drinking water and correcting the diet. But if the brain is already affected, chances of a cure are slim. The staggering motions will keep recurring.

Prevent the outbreak of this disease by feeding your birds pelleted diets or commercial seed mixes that are well supplemented.

Overgrown Claws

Symptoms: The claws grow too long, and birds are no longer able to get a good hold on perches. They have trouble standing up and easily get caught in the grating of the cage or aviary, where they may get stuck and die from hanging upside down.

Cause: The perches are too thin and smooth, and the claws, which grow continually, have no chance to wear down properly.

This is the proper way to hold a bird for cutting the claws.

Treatment: Cut the claws with sharp scissors. Be careful not to injure the blood vessels. You can see them shine through the nail darkly when you hold the foot up against a light. To prevent overgrowth, use perches of the proper thickness and rough natural branches in the cage or aviary.

This bird's claws are overgrown.

Overgrown or Crossed Bill

Symptoms: In an overgrown bill, the maxilla is abnormally elongated. In a crossed bill, the maxilla or mandible grows to one side and either up or down so much that the bird is prevented from taking up food properly.

Cause: There is insufficient opportunity for the bill, which keeps growing, to be worn down.

Treatment: Trim the bill carefully with sharp scissors. In the case of an overgrown bill, cut the longer mandible to fit the shorter one. If the bill is crossed, try to trim it to the original shape. Do not injure the underlying bone, because otherwise, the horny tissue will no longer grow properly or at all and the bird will have trouble eating.

Prevent deformations of the bill by placing several rough natural branches in the cage or aviary. This gives the birds a chance to keep their bills in shape.

A well-balanced pelleted diet also helps prevent abnormal growth of the bill. Consult your avian veterinarian.

Plucked Feathers

Symptoms: Feathers missing on the head and neck.

Cause: Feather picking of cage-mates can result from overcrowding, nesting site fights, inappropriate sexual aggression, or sickness. Picking is typically seen around the head and neck of affected birds. Unaddressed picking can lead to cannibalism, especially with Zebra Finches.

Treatment: Picked birds should be separated, examined, given extra heat, and taken to the veterinarian to address skin trauma and possible underlying disease. Preventive measures include increasing cage space, nest sites, and materials; improving diet; and providing multiple food and water bowls.

Prevention Is Best

All exotic finches are relatively small birds. They have a high metabolism, which means that they have to keep eating continually and that they use up energy fast. That is why their overall health deteriorates rapidly if they get sick. It is very important to check all birds for signs of illness every day. Even careful observation may detect an illness too late for veterinary help to be effective. This is good reason for making every possible effort to try to prevent disease. The best way to do this is to feed the birds a healthy diet of absolutely clean food containing plenty of vitamins and calcium and to be painstakingly hygienic in the preparation of food and in the maintenance of the cages and aviaries.

Even if you have kept exotic finches for some time, you should always consult an avian veterinarian for the diagnosis and treatment of your sick birds. Find a veterinarian who is used to treating finches before an acute need for his or her service arises, and have well-bird examinations done.

Chapter Seven

Understanding Exotic Finches

To insure and expand the available food supply, primitive humans started as early as 10,000 or 12,000 years ago to take wild animals out of their natural habitat and keep them nearby to use. Gradually, humans learned to exercise control over them, and from this beginning, the habit of keeping pets developed. Birds have always been favorites. Their daytime activities, varied songs, and the infinite variety of color combinations in their plumage have always fascinated people.

Today, exotic finches, along with parrots and parakeets, are among the most popular cage birds. Exotic finches do not sing as much or as melodiously as many other songbirds; their song is rather quiet and insignificant. But they make up for this by their lovely coloration and markings. Exotic finches are lively, sociable, and—for the most part—peaceable. They are fairly easy to care for, and produce offspring relatively quickly and reliably.

If you want to meet the needs of your exotic finches successfully, you will have to learn to recognize and interpret typical behavior. This chapter is designed to help you do just that—namely, to help you gain an understanding of exotic finches.

The Finch Family

Exotic finches, many scientists believe, go back about 30 million years, to the end of the Miocene period. They are members of the family Estrildidae—waxbills and allies—that consists of about 128 species and forms part of the suborder Passeres, or songbirds, in the order of Passeriformes (passerines, or perching birds). One of the features that distinguish songbirds from other birds is the structure of the syrinx, the vocal organ of birds. Close relatives of the exotic finches are the whydahs and the African and Asian weavers.

Estrildidae finches—which we call "exotic finches"—differ from finches of the family Fringillidae by the number of primary feathers—Estrildidae have ten, Fringillidae only nine—and in nest-building behavior—Fringillidae females take exclusive charge of nest building and incubation but the Estrildidae parents share these chores.

Weavers (family Ploceidae), which are found in Africa and throughout southern Asia and Indochina, differ from both the above families in the behavior associated with breeding. The male weaver builds several round nests before starting his courtship song, and he offers them to the female to pick from. All the female has to do is pad the nest and lay her eggs. Many male weavers have several females simultaneously and are thus polygamous.

Bird Anatomy

Feathers: Birds are vertebrates and differ from all other classes of animals by being covered with feathers. There are two kinds of feathers: down feathers, which serve for warmth and make up the young birds' first plumage, and contour feathers, which serve as an unbroken covering for the entire body. A typical feather consists of a central shaft, or rachis, from which barbs branch out on both sides, forming the vane. The primary and secondary wing feathers and the tail feathers are used for propulsion and to control flight.

All feathers are made up of a horny substance; they may have evolved from the scales of birds' reptilian ancestors. Once feathers are fully formed, they are no longer supplied with blood and are therefore made up of dead tissue. Weather and use gradually wear them down, and in order to be able to fly, birds

If you want to take good care of your finches, you'll have to understand their behavior.

Flight

Exotic finches that come from regions with dense vegetation fly only in short spurts. The path of their flight is slightly arched (firefinches of the genus *Lagonosticta* and Cordon-bleus). Cutthroats, Zebra Finches, Long-tailed Grassfinches, and other species that live in an open landscape fly in great arches. Exotic finches that live in the reeds can synchronize turns and other flight maneuvers in a flock, all the birds flying in the same rhythm.

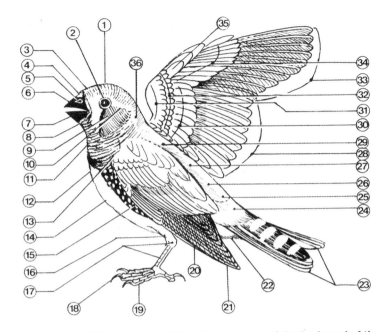

What is what on a finch? Knowing what the different parts of the body and of the plumage are called is especially useful when talking to the veterinarian.

1. Crown
2. Eye
3. Forehead
4. Cere
5. Nostril
6. Upper mandible
7. Lower mandible
8. Chin
9. Cheek
10. Auricular region
11. Throat
12. Breast
13. Shoulder

14. Belly
15. Side
16. Lower leg
17. Ankle or tarsus
    (above), middle foot
    (below)
18. Toenail
19. Toe
20. Cloaca
21. Primaries
22. Under tail coverts
23. Tail
24. Upper tail coverts

25. Rump
26. Lower back
27. Back
28. Secondaries
29. Upper back
30. Secondary coverts
31. Marginal wing coverts
32. Secondary and lesser
    wing coverts
33. Primaries
34. Primary coverts
35. Bastard wing
36. Nape or neck

have to get rid of old feathers and grow new ones every year. This process, which is controlled by hormonal action, is called molting.

Forelimbs: The forelimbs of birds have in the course of evolution been modified into wings. In some species, such as the ostrich and the emu, it is

supposed that the wings later lost their special function because these birds had no predators they had to escape by flight. The wing muscles and feathers are much modified in these birds.

Plumage: Plumage serves not only to regulate body temperature but also to give a bird's body the characteristic streamlined shape that is so advantageous for flying.

Body temperature: Birds, like mammals, are warm-blooded. In contrast to reptiles and amphibians, which take on the temperature of their environment, birds maintain a constant body temperature of 104°F (40°C) and can therefore inhabit colder regions. Fluctuations in external temperature are, to some extent, compensated for by the plumage. If it is cold, the birds fluff themselves up, and the additional air between the feathers serves as insulation. But small species such as our exotic finches can withstand temperature fluctuations only to a limited degree. If the temperature drops below a certain point for an extended period, they may die of cold.

Since birds have no sweat glands, they open their beaks and pant if they get overheated. The moisture in the buccal cavity evaporates, producing a cooling effect.

Respiratory System

The skeleton of a bird is very light because some of the bones are not all solid but are hollow and are connected to a system of air sacs. Air sacs in the breast area are connected to the bronchial system of the lungs, a fairly complex structure of tubes. These tubes branch off from two main bronchi along the back and abdomen and subdivide further. The finest tubes are surrounded by minute blood vessels through which an active exchange of gases takes place. When the bird inhales, the air passes through the lungs to the air sacs; when it exhales, the air moves back along the same path. The air passes through the blood vessels twice, thus allowing the bird to absorb oxygen more effectively and to fly long distances.

Color of Plumage

Many songbirds, among them the exotic finches, have conspicuously bright colors. The coloration and markings of the plumage often function as signals for other members of the species; generally, only the easily visible parts of the plumage are brightly colored, while the hidden ones such as the down feathers or the lower parts of the body are whitish or gray. But what gives feathers their color?

If a feather is cut in half, one can see through a microscope that there is an outer, ring-shaped horny, or keratinous, layer that encloses many small chambers filled with air. These

Finches are among the most brightly colored birds in the world.

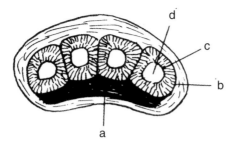

Cross-section of a bird feather: a) Dark ground; b) Outer keratinous layer; c) Wall of empty chamber; d) Inside of chamber.

tiny chambers contain various kinds of pigments. Melanin is responsible for dark coloration, and carotenoid pigments give rise to yellowish and reddish colors. Bright yellows and reds are produced by various lipochrome pigments.

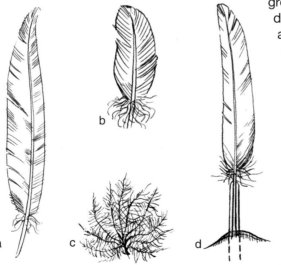

Types of feathers: a) Primary of left wing; b) Contour feather; c) Down feather; d) Growing feather with blood supply in shaft.

The color blue, however, is not created by a stored pigment but rather is what is called a structural color. Empty keratine chambers sit on a dark ground, and this makes the feather appear blue. If there is an outer layer of yellow keratine surrounding the air chambers and the dark layer behind them, the feather appears green to the human eye.

In white feathers, both the dark ground behind the air chambers and the yellow coloration of the outer keratine layer are absent. In feathers that appear blackish, thick clusters of melanin grains are present.

All feathers wear out in the course of time. Light-colored ones are less durable than dark ones and wear out more quickly.

If a bird gets sick when molting or growing its juvenile plumage, or if it does not get proper nourishment at these times, the feathers will show malformations, the so-called hunger jags.

Molting

The change of feathers is called molting. In most birds, it takes place at least once a year, after mating and rearing the young. The process begins when new feathers form underneath the old ones—like the new teeth below the baby teeth in a child—and gradually push them out.

All exotic finches except for one wear the same bright plumage all year-round; the exception is the male Avadavat, which is bright scarlet during mating season and afterwards changes to an unobtrusive brown similar to that of the female. Exotic finches do not lose all their feathers at once when they molt; instead, new ones grow in as others fall out. Still, the birds are somewhat less active and more sensitive to changes in temperature during molting than they are otherwise since the renewal of plumage places a strain on the metabolic system. This is the reason—in addition to hormonal activity—why exotic finches never enter the mating season during molt. Sick birds do not molt. You can consequently assume that your new birds are healthy if they start to molt after a period of acclimation in a new aviary.

Sense Organs

Birds orient themselves primarily by sight.

Sight: The vast majority of birds have predominately monocular vision, with varying degrees of binocular vision depending on the species. For example, owls' eyes face forward, giving them the keenest binocular vision of all avian species.

The eyeball of a bird is also quite mobile. While in the human eye the eyeball moves back and forth between the lids, the pupils of birds' eyes always stay in the middle. Humans and most other mammals close their eyes by lowering the upper eyelid. In birds, the lower lid can rise up. Birds also have a third eyelid—a nicitating membrane below the lower lid that they move across the cornea from the inner side of the eye outward; it helps to protect the eye.

Hearing: All species of birds have a very well-developed sense of hearing. A bird's ear is basically the same as that of a mammal except that it lacks the pinna, or outer ear.

Smell: Unlike most mammals, the majority of birds do not have a very acute sense of smell. Exceptions here are the New World vultures, many seabirds, and the kiwi of New Zealand. These birds find their food, in part, by smell, which they also use to orient themselves.

Taste: A bird's taste buds are located on the back of the tongue, underneath the tongue, on the soft palate, and on the upper epiglottis. Generally, birds do not taste food with the beak or the tip of the tongue.

Body Language

Birds, like humans, express their feelings and moods in many ways. If you take the time to watch your birds intently, you will soon recognize various postures and understand their meaning.

Sleeping Posture

The sleeping posture of exotic finches is like that of other songbirds: They may pull their heads in between their shoulders, but more frequently they turn their heads back and tuck their bills under their wings.

This is the sleeping posture of finches: The head is pulled in between the shoulders or turned back and tucked in under the wing.

They may fluff up their feathers somewhat and pull one leg up close to the body. A special arrangement of the tendons and muscles in the legs keeps birds from tumbling to the ground while sleeping. When the knee and ankle are bent in the normal sleeping position, the toes automatically grip.

Normally, diurnally active birds, such as the exotic finches, do not nap at all during the day but sleep very soundly at night. If you catch a bird napping during the day, you should keep an eye on it because this is usually a sign of illness.

Exotic finches can be divided according to their sleeping habits into perch sleepers and nest sleepers. Birds of the first group spend the night perching on a branch in the position described above, either singly or huddled together. Nest sleepers build nests for sleeping even

outside of the mating period. These birds should always be given the opportunity to build nests because they easily catch cold at night. Generally, only one pair of birds or a group of siblings will sleep in such a nest. Spice Finches, Bronze Mannikins, and Bicheno Finches are the only species that sometimes sleep in larger groups. The largest number of birds observed in one nest was 17 Spice Finches.

Fright Position

Often shape alone will tell you how a bird is feeling. A bird that is sick sits on its perch all fluffed up, often with eyes closed. A frightened bird, on the other hand, will try to sit straight up and make itself as thin and "invisible" as possible, especially if other occupants of the aviary

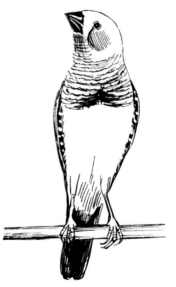

Slim with fright: The bird sits straight up, feathers flattened tight against the body.

or cage have been chasing it a lot. It will hide in a corner and lay down its feathers as flat as it can. Birds that are really at ease neither fluff themselves up nor sit unnaturally straight up. They hop around or look relaxed on their perches.

Grooming

Intact plumage is crucial to the survival of all birds, because body warmth is maintained only if the feathers are in top condition. Birds condition their plumage by preening themselves every day. They clean and smooth out their large wing and tail feathers by pulling them through the beak one by one. The smaller feathers, too, are kept in shape and arranged properly with the beak. Since birds cannot reach the back of the neck, the cheeks, and the top of the head with their beaks, they scratch these parts of the body with their toes. They raise one leg at a time, spread the wing of the same side, pass the leg up over the wing, and reach across the shoulder from behind. Other types of birds, such as pigeons, scratch from the front: They do not spread the wing but stretch the leg straight forward.

Preening: Every so often, preening birds fluff up their feathers a little and then shake themselves. This causes all the feathers to lie down in their proper position. Birds like to preen themselves with special thoroughness after a bath.

To keep the feathers elastic and water-resistant, birds lubricate them with a fatty substance secreted by

Finches groom themselves by fluffing up their feathers.

the preening gland. This gland is located on the lower back just above the base of the tail. There they pick up the secretion with their bills and distribute it over the feathers. The parts of the head that are out of

Preening: The bird arranges the feathers properly by drawing each one through its bill.

range for the bill are lubricated by bending and twisting the head in such a way that it rubs against the already treated parts of the plumage.

Bathing

In the wild, different kinds of exotic finches show different needs for bathing.

• Cherry, Gouldian, and Zebra Finches and all munias like to take a bath several times a day, while finches of the genus *Poephila* (Long-tailed Grassfinch, Parson Finch, and Masked Grassfinch) bathe only in the morning and evening and are thus less dependent on water.

• Crimson Finches wet their feathers only with the moisture on foliage.

• Star Finches and Bicheno Finches like to clean themselves in light rain and make use, particularly after extended dry periods, of water sprinklers in towns and suburbs. They keep flying through the spray of water until they are soaked.

• In northern and central Australia, exotic finches start to take baths with the rainy season.

Observation both in the wild and in aviaries shows that one bathing bird moves others to join in. Some birds often have to wait because the shallow area is not large enough for all of them. But the need to bathe is so great, or the stimulus so powerful, that these birds begin to go through bathing motions on the dry ground.

Exotic finches all love the sun and like to sunbathe every day if possible. They spread their tails and raise their feathers so that as much sunlight as possible can reach the skin.

Tail Movements

In some species, body movements are always accompanied by a whipping of the tail. This motion of the tail can express excitement, alarm, or the intention to take off. The tail whips up and down when the bird lands on a perch, and it wags sideways when the body turns. In some species this wagging is not necessarily accompanied by body movements. Exotic finches also twitch their wings, which probably signals intent to fly away.

In ground-dwelling species the tail movements are less pronounced than in those that live in trees and bushes. Masked Grassfinches whip their tails slightly when landing on a perch, but closely related species do not do this. Some exotic finches, such as the Bicheno, the Crimson, the Star, the Painted, and the Spice Finch, sometimes spread their tails, which is also a sign of excitement.

Eating

What kinds of food specific exotic finches need and how they eat the various seeds is discussed in Chapter Eight, Descriptions of Exotic Finches.

Seeds: If exotic finches want to dig up a seed that is buried in the ground, they get rid of the earth around it as other seedeaters do by slashing at it from side to side with a closed bill. They always shell seeds by moving the lower mandible rapidly against the upper one while the tongue pushes the seed into proper position. Mealworms are worked on similarly, as is nesting material.

Insects: Many exotic finches also eat insects. When raising their young, birds need a lot more food; Star Finches, Crimson Finches, and Cutthroats live almost entirely on insects during this time. But how do they catch the insects? Star Finches and some others pick them off leaves, while Gouldian and Pictorella Finches eat them off the ground. Many other species sally from a perch. They first spot their prey, then catch it in flight, and return to their perch.

The most common prey of some finches, such as the Bronze Mannikin and Cordon-bleus, are flying termites and ants. The birds do not bother chewing these insects but swallow them whole. If the insects are too large, they are reduced to bite size in a few chomps. After each feeding, the birds clean their bills by wiping them against something.

Drinking: Certain Australian species have a special way of drinking. Most exotic finches drink like chickens—that is, they raise their beaks each time they take up water and let the water run down their throats. The Diamond Firetail, Star Finch, Gouldian Finch, Zebra Finch, Bicheno Finch, Masked Grassfinch, Parson Finch, and Long-tailed Grassfinch can drink without raising the head for every swallow. This allows them to drink water from very tiny puddles and to spend less time at watering places, where they may be threatened by small predatory birds. The ability to suck up water also allows them to penetrate further into arid regions. Presumably, this method of drinking was first adopted by the birds for drinking dew off leaves.

Long-tailed Grassfinches, Parson Finches, and Masked Grassfinches are the only exotic finches that are able to drop down to the water directly from steep banks. All other Australian finches can drink only in shallow water. Because of their special skill, the three species just mentioned can take advantage of watering troughs set up for cattle in dry inland areas. Zebra, Cherry, Gouldian, and Bicheno Finches fly to the water about once every hour. Long-tailed Grassfinches, Parson Finches, and Masked Grassfinches drink only in the morning and evening and may range long distances from their watering places during the day.

Communal Behavior

If you watch exotic finches for any length of time, you will notice pairs of birds that keep each other constant company. They fly to the water and forage for food together, preen each other, and rest together. You may be sure that these are pairs that stay together past the breeding

Sound is the primary form of communication among finches.

season and have formed a bond that is more or less permanent, depending on the species. Most exotic finches are gregarious birds that always live together with others of their kind. That is why exotic finches should never be kept singly. They need very close contact with a partner; otherwise, they pine away.

Sounds

All exotic finches communicate with one another through sounds. African mannikins, African and Indian silverbills, the true waxbills (those of the genus *Estrilda*), Long-tailed and Masked Grassfinches, Parson, Bicheno, Zebra, Star, and Gouldian Finches, and some munias emit two "contact" calls: The softer contact call serves to keep the immediate neighbors of a flock together; the louder call is used to keep the whole flock together or to maintain contact between mates that are at some distance from each other.

Beyond this, exotic finches communicate by emitting calls of warning or aggression and calls to attract a mate or offspring to the nest.

Sitting and Grooming

The strong social needs of exotic finches are clearly expressed in two patterns of behavior: huddling next to each other (contact sitting) and mutual grooming. Different species display this behavior in various degrees.

Contact sitting: All munias, the Chestnut-breasted Finch, the Yellow-rumped Finch, the Masked Grass-finch, and some African waxbills practice *contact sitting* in long rows. Long-tailed Grassfinches and Parson and Zebra Finches sit only in pairs. Crimson Finches and Star Finches limit contact sitting to the mating season. And then there are some species that avoid physical contact with others as much as possible. Among these are the Painted, Pictorella, and Goudlian Finches as well as all Parrot Finches. These birds sit closely together only as juveniles and keep at a distance from each other once they reach sexual maturity.

The reasons for this varying need for physical contact are not altogether clear. Since it occurs among some finches of tropical regions, contact sitting apparently does not arise simply from the need to keep warm.

Mutual grooming: This behavior plays a central role in the lives of many exotic finches and is absent only in those birds that sit together without physical contact, such as the Painted, the Pictorella, and the Goudlian Finch. In mutual grooming, only those parts of the body that the bird can scratch but not properly preen are offered—that is, the head, the throat, and the back of the neck. One of a pair of birds sitting next to each other will raise the feathers on its head or neck and turn the area of the body it would like to have groomed toward the partner, which will then draw each feather of the indicated spot through its bill. If the bill happens to touch some other part of the body, the bird submitting to the grooming immediately gets

This way of huddling together is called "contact sitting."

nervous and either pecks at its partner or flies away.

Pintailed Parrot Finches bend toward each other and gently groom each other without snuggling up. Long-tailed Grassfinches, Parson, Cherry, and Zebra Finches always pair up for grooming with the same bird, just as they do for contact sitting. Other contact-hungry species (Spice Finch, Yellow-rumped Finch, and Masked Grassfinch—those species that contact sit in rows) will pair up for grooming with any member of the flock.

In the wild, exotic finches engage in mutual grooming and contact sitting only with members of their own species. In captivity, their need for contact can be so great that, when there is no bird of their kind present, they will seek out a partner of a different species. If at all possible, they choose closely related birds that

Finches groom each other frequently.

have similar courting rituals and calls and are therefore relatively easy to communicate with.

Such a mixed pair of closely related exotic finches as, for instance, a Rosy-rumped and a Black-rumped Waxbill, may stick together even when the aviculturist later introduces other members of the same species into the aviary. The attachment between the two birds may have grown so strong that a "stranger," even if it belongs to the proper species, is not readily accepted. Even if the keeper separates the two partners and houses each with a member of its own species, it may be a while before a new bond develops. Mixed matches between birds that are not so closely related dissolve much more easily when other members of the "right" species appear on the scene.

Aggressive Behavior

Although exotic finches are extremely sociable, birds of this family do sometimes quarrel. This is true even of couples. Recently formed pairs fight the most. Males and females participate equally in conflicts, the males biting females and young birds without inhibition.

Exotic finches fight over all sorts of things: a female, a perch, nesting material, a good nesting site, a sleeping nest, or a sleeping perch.

Threatening: The mildest form of aggression is simple *threatening*. Most exotic finches threaten their opponents by extending the neck forward slightly with open bill (munias and Cherry Finch) or silently with closed bill. Some African species, such as the Cutthroat, accompany this behavior with a long, threatening sound.

The fighting behavior of all species is relatively simple and shows only slight variations. There are two basic patterns: the pecking fight and the ousting fight.

Pecking: In a *pecking fight* caused by some minor conflict, the birds sit opposite each other and hack at each other with their beaks, trying to get a hold of the opponent's head or breast feathers. Some especially gregarious munias have evolved a more innocuous variant and fight only symbolically by pecking at each other's bills, often not even moving apart. At a further stage of evolution, it is possible that this pecking, thought to be symbolic, changed to the even milder threatening behavior described above.

In pecking fights, some species try to intimidate their opponents by displaying the dramatic markings of their plumage or by raising their feathers in special ways: Zebra Finches flatten their crown feathers; Painted Finches spread their tails wide; Crimson Finches also spread their bright red tails and at the same time puff up their crown feathers. In particularly vehement fights between two Crimson Finches, one of the birds also raises the wing away from the opponent straight up in the air to make itself appear bigger. In Magpie and Bronze Mannikins, this raising of the wing accompanies every pecking fight and has become a threatening gesture.

Ousting: An *ousting fight* is more serious. One bird will fly up to another, chase it off its perch, pursue it, and rout it again every time it tries to settle. A pecking fight can turn into an ousting fight when the loser gives up its place and flees. Ousting fights occur primarily in conflicts over territory during mating season. At this time the male of a pair will attack any intruder of his own species, as well as other exotic finches, without a preliminary pecking fight.

Sometimes an ousting fight can turn into a regular air battle in which the two opponents grapple each other in the air, tails spread wide, and sometimes drop to the ground in each other's grip. But such fierce fighting occurs only when males of similar strength compete for a female or a nesting site. Much more normal are the regular ousting fights described above.

Some species favor one or the other method of fighting: Star Finches, munias, and Gouldian Finches usually have pecking fights while the Crimson Finch, Long-tailed Grassfinch, Zebra Finch, Parson Finch, Bicheno Finch, and Masked Grassfinch usually engage in ousting fights.

Gestures of submission: Along with aggressive behavior, all social animals have developed gestures of mollification and submission to make coexistence possible. But among exotic finches, gestures of submission have been observed in only a few species. These are Java Sparrows, Long-tailed Grassfinches, Zebra, Parson, and Gouldian Finches, and Masked Grassfinches. Here the weaker bird that has been attacked uses the begging motions of a baby bird to appease its attacker. Presumably, losers in a conflict also try to mollify their opponents by assuming the mutual grooming position.

Frequency of fights: The frequency with which fights occur also varies from species to species and is not always directly related to the degree of sociability. Mating Crimson Finches constantly fight others once they enter mating season and attack birds of other species as well, even ones as large as pigeons. But Star Finches, the gregarious Spice Finches, Gouldian Finches, and Parson Finches also fight quite a lot.

If you observe that one of your exotic finches is constantly chased by one or several of its companions and that they let it neither eat nor rest, you have to catch it and move it to another cage or aviary; otherwise, the bird may die of heart failure brought on by stress.

Finch Songs

In contrast to the music of many other songbirds, the singing of exotic finches lacks distinction. Since song is used neither to assert territory nor to challenge other males, but is directed exclusively at the female, it is soft and cannot be heard far away. The only exceptions we know are the males of the Common Waxbill and the Bar-breasted Firefinch, whose song can take on a clearly combative note. If they want to drive away a rival, they do it by singing loudly.

The songs of the different species of exotic finches vary so much that no general description can be given that would apply to all of them. Some are flutelike, some more twittering or chirping, and others are more of a throaty roll. Each species has its characteristic tone.

When a male courts a female, he sings. In a number of species, the male holds a long blade of grass in his bill while singing. This ritualized gesture indicates to the female that the male is ready to join her in building a nest and rearing young.

In most species, only the males sing, and listening to the birds is the best method for determining their sex. This is true for all munias, for all Australian finches, and for waxbills of the genus *Estrilda*. In other species, however, such as Violet-eared Waxbills, Purple Grenadiers, Melba Finches, and some firefinches of the genus *Lagonosticta*, the females can sing, too, if they are without a mate. But the song of these females is shorter, softer, and less elaborate than that of the males and also less frequent. Female Purple Grenadiers and female Violet-eared Waxbills break into loud song when they are separated from their mates by force. This is an attempt to maintain or reestablish contact with their partners.

An interesting phenomenon can be observed in a number of exotic finches, especially in munias, some Australian species such as the Gouldian, Star, and Cherry Finches, the African Silverbill, and the Cutthroat. Two to three birds will gather closely around a singing male and listen to him intently. They will lean their heads next to the bill of the singing bird as though trying to catch every last detail. There seem to be some especially popular individuals that are surrounded by listeners all the time while other males are ignored.

Pair Formation

Pairing and courtship display are closely linked and cannot be treated separately from each other, especially since they are often characterized by the same activities.

In many species of exotic finches pairs form in the flock long before the mating season starts. In such cases, the male and female always stay close to each other and do things together.

The male takes the initiative in trying to form a pair by approaching a female while singing and performing courtship rituals. If the female is ready to accept the male, she welcomes him or engages in courtship behavior too. If she already has a mate or is unwilling to pair up, she chases away the courting male or flies off. If the female is interested, the male approaches her again and again until one day the two of them perch next to each other, and the female grooms the male. From this point on, they can be considered a permanent pair.

It also happens that a female flies up to a male, greets him, and urges him to sing. The male, whether already paired off or not, goes through his role as described above, but if he already has a mate, his interest soon flags. Bicheno Finches, Spice Finches, and Bronze Mannikins start concentrating their mutual grooming more and more on the chosen partners at the onset of mating season, and gradually the pairs shift their allegiance away from the flock. This way of pairing off seems to predominate among those species where the plumage of the two sexes is undifferentiated.

Unattached male Crimson Finches leave the flock when the mating season approaches, position themselves near a good nesting site, and emit "long-distance" calls to nest. If an unpaired female responds, the males court her. Female Star and Crimson Finches can also take the initiative and invite their own partners or strange males to court them. To do this, the female Star Finch holds a long blade of grass in her bill and woos the male. He then starts to sing to her or engage in courtship displays.

Courtship Displays

Exotic finches have elaborate courtship rituals that differ from species to species and help prevent crossbreeding. Since there are so many different patterns of behavior, we can here describe only the most common ones.

Grass display: In the firefinches and waxbills of the genera *Lagonosticta* and *Estrilda*, the male finds a long blade of grass (or a feather), picks it up by one end, and takes it to the female, which sits perched up on a branch. There he puffs up his abdominal feathers, turns his tail toward the female, whips up and down a few times on the branch without letting go, and begins to sing. This *grass display* ritual tells the female that he wants to build a nest with her and raise a family. In many species, the link between tangible use and symbolic meaning of the grass display has gotten lost. Spice Finches and White-backed Munias and one kind of munia from Java still pick up blades of grass when they get ready to court, but they drop them again before they start singing. Some closely related Australian birds of the genus *Lonchura* and Asiatic munias dispense with the grass altogether, as do the Long-tailed Grassfinch, the Parson Finch, the Bicheno Finch, and the Zebra Finch. One does occasionally see the grass display among immature Long-tailed Grassfinches but never among adult ones, which seems to indicate that the species once fol-

A male Common Waxbill performing the grass display ritual. He is signaling to the female that he would like to build a nest and raise a family with her. Sometimes feathers are used instead of grass.

lowed this behavior pattern but later abandoned it.

Bob-ups: In various African species, the female, too, courts her partner with a blade of grass in her bill, especially if he is not very active. In a few species the males *bob up* while going through the grass display ritual. This behavior is particularly obvious in waxbills, Purple Grenadiers, Peter's and Green Twinspots, and firefinches of the genus *Lagonosticta*. In "bob-ups," the birds push their heads up and forward in time with their leg movements. This bobbing up is similar to the motions the male goes through when building the ceiling of the nest out of grass.

Bowing: The courtship display of the Diamond Firetail is also impressive: "Here, too, the male looks for an especially long blade of grass and, holding it in his beak, he flies up to a flexible horizontal branch. There he starts to whip up and down, keeping firm hold of the branch with his toes, and sings his strange song consisting of a series of short bass notes. If the female approaches, he turns toward her halfway and increases the speed and force of his whipping. Finally, he bends down and forward, twists his head in such a way that he peers up at her sideways, and wags his head the way baby birds begging for food do. This performance seems to have a magic effect on the female. Thus, the male first woos the female with his courtship dance and the nesting symbol and then playacts the hungry nestling, appealing to the female's maternal instincts, which are acti-

The male finch courts the female finch during the formation of mating pairs.

vated in the mating season" (Nicolai, 1976).

Although not as pronounced as in the Diamond Firetail, this *bowing* before the female is also characteristic of several African species such as the Dybowski and the Green Twinspots, the Violet-eared Waxbill, the Purple Grenadier, the three Cordon-bleus, the waxbills of the genus *Estrilda*, the mannikins, and the Avadavat and Green Avadavat.

Bending down: Australian finches—Star, Crimson, and Zebra Finches—and munias exhibit a behavior similar to, though not exactly like, the bowing just described. The males *bend down* before the females and brush their bills back and forth. These gestures, too, are reminiscent of rearing behavior. Before the parent birds fly to the nest to feed their young, they always brush their bills against the ground to get rid of seed husks that are harmful for the young.

Singing: In species where the grass display ritual has been dropped, *song* has gained in importance and has become the main method of courting. Male Cutthroats, for instance, sing to their females while jerking their heads from side to side. When getting more excited, the male Cutthroat, like the *Lagonosticta* firefinches during their grass display ritual, whips up, angling the ankle joint when turning from side to side.

Mating

It is often stated that the courtship song or display is followed by mating. But females only rarely respond to a mate's courting by assuming the typical female *mating position*. More commonly, the female is the one to indicate readiness to mate to the male that is sitting calmly next to her and that may not have performed the courtship display recently.

By squatting down in front of the male and vibrating her tail, this female is signaling to him that she is ready to mate.

In species that mate outside the nest, the female crouches before the male and vibrates her tail quickly up and down. Diamond Firetails, Gouldian Finches, Cutthroats, Avadavats, and all members of the genus *Estrilda* mate in their nests.

Nesting Sites

Choosing a proper nesting site is crucial for all birds because it largely determines whether the young will survive or not. Most exotic finches know instinctively what makes for a good nesting site, but the females have a clearer sense than the males, who will quite often pick inappropriate sites.

Exotic finches, such as Gouldian Finches, which sometimes nest in holes in trees when living in the wild, will in captivity readily accept half-open or enclosed nesting boxes. Other species, such as the Violet-eared Waxbill and the Melba Finch, generally ignore artificial nesting sites and build their nests only in a thicket of low branches. Still other species, such as the Aurora Finch, nest only in bushes and trees in the wild but accept nesting boxes in captivity.

The male and the female work together in the search for a nesting site. The male hops ahead of the female and suggests various places. When he has found a particularly promising spot, he crouches there, moves his body from side to side on bent legs, and calls to the female with the typical nesting call. If the female approves of the site, she follows the male and behaves similarly. Should the spot not meet her fancy, she pays no attention or hops away. Then the male starts looking again. The female herself never picks a site; she merely inspects what he has found and then decides.

Once the site is picked, the male goes off to find nesting material, and both partners start building the nest on the chosen site while making nesting calls. In most species, the male collects the nesting material, and the female turns it into a nest.

Finches choose their nest sites carefully.

Rooster nest: Some species of exotic finches build a second, bowl-shaped nest, the so-called *rooster nest* on top of their regular spherical brood nest. It used to be thought that the male spent the night in this rooster nest during the incubating period, but since we now know that the male joins the brooding female in the regular nest at night, it seems that the function of the rooster nest may be to confuse enemies, especially tree snakes.

The Mating Season

Food is not available in the same quantities and quality year-round for birds living in nature. But to raise their young, birds need a steady supply of nutritious food in order to meet the great energy needs of their offspring. This is why the mating and rearing period of all birds is when food is available in greatest abundance. Just when this happens in the yearly cycle depends on external factors such as length of day and weather, as well as on internal ones such as hormonal activities. Exotic finches need large amounts of live insects or ripening seeds to feed their young, and these are found in abundance only during and shortly after the rainy season.

• Birds such as the Orange-winged Pytilia and the Melba Finch that feed primarily on insects breed early in the rainy season since this is when there are the most insects.

• The seeds of grasses do not begin to ripen until the latter half of the rainy season and early in the dry period that follows, and that is why species that raise their offspring mainly on seeds—species such as the Quail Finch and Goldbreast—postpone mating until the latter part of the rainy season.

• Bar-breasted Firefinches and Jameson's Firefinches breed as late as the first quarter of the dry period.

• Two African species, the Aurora Finch and the Yellow-winged Pytilia, mate only in the dry season and do not start building their nests until several weeks after the last rainfalls.

The timing of the rainy and the dry seasons varies considerably from region to region in Africa. In southern Africa, the months of November and December are the rainy season; in the western parts of the continent, as in eastern Nigeria, the rainy season falls in the months of May to October. In the arid sections of Australia, the rainy periods are not as regular and predictable as in Africa, and the birds there consequently have to be prepared to mate at any time to be able to take advantage of the food supplies that follow sudden rainfalls. Under these conditions, even one heavy shower may be sufficient to start the birds going on their courtship rituals and nest building. In these species, such as Zebra Finches, the fledglings stay in the nest for only a short time and reach independence and sexual maturity earlier than other exotic finches. Whether or not these birds raise a second brood later in the year depends on the length of the rainy season.

During the dry season, when food and water are scarce, many exotic finches form flocks that range far seeking food. The flocks stay together until the onset of mating season, when pairs of birds ready to breed go off to look for nesting sites.

Among the African finches it is primarily the Common Waxbill, the Orange-cheeked Waxbill, and the African Silverbill that live in flocks, and among the Australian ones, the Gouldian and the Pictorella Finches. Other species, such as the Melba Finch and the Purple Grenadier, stay in pairs year-round and do not form flocks.

Brood Hosts

Under some of the entries in Chapter Eight, Descriptions of Exotic Finches, a species of whydah is mentioned that acts as a brood parasite to a particular kind of finch. Whydahs are distributed over the savannas and steppes of Africa. The name "whydah" comes from a town in Nigeria by the same name where the birds are common, but they are also often called widowbirds because of the long, usually black, tail feathers of the male's mating plumage. Female whydahs do not build nests of their own during the mating period but instead search out nests of exotic finches that do not yet contain the full number of eggs, where the female whydahs deposit their eggs. Each species of whydah always acts as a parasite to the same species of finch: The Shaft-tailed Whydah picks nests of the Violet-eared Waxbill; the Pintailed Whydah, those of the Common Waxbill; and the Togo Paradise Whydah, those of the Yellow-winged Pytilia.

The baby whydah hatches either shortly before or along with its nestmates, but, unlike the cuckoo, another brood parasite, it does not throw them, or other eggs, out of the nest. Instead, it grows up along with the young finches.

The nestlings of exotic finches have a bold pattern of dark spots and lines in the buccal cavity that simulates the parent birds to feed them. Baby whydahs have a mouth

Violet-eared Waxbills (a male is shown building the nest) act as brood hosts to Shaft-tailed Whydahs (male, upper left; female, lower left).

pattern that exactly matches that of their nestmates and as a result, they do not draw negative attention to themselves. They also mimic the begging calls and postures of the baby finches, as well as their first plumage. Thus, the finch parents are unable to distinguish the intruder from their own offspring and raise it along with their young. Since each species of exotic finches has its own specific buccal markings and begging notes, each kind of whydah has to specialize and copy its host perfectly. If, for some reason, a whydah egg has been placed in the nest of the "wrong" kind of finch, the hatchling is immediately detected as a stranger and thrown out.

As they grow up, the young whydahs learn the songs, calls, and other important behavior patterns, both male and female, of their hosts, and this enables them later, when they are mature, to find a pair of the right kind of exotic finches and to smuggle their eggs into the nest.

Whydah Songs

All male whydahs know two repertories of songs: their own and that of "their" finches. The first consists of harsh, screeching sounds that are fairly similar among all whydahs; it is inborn and does not have to be learned. But mixed in with this first repertory are all the motifs and elements that make up the song of the host finch species. A male why-

Wydah females place their eggs in the nests of exotic finches.

dah trying to intimidate a rival uses his whydah calls, but when he woos a female, he sings the songs he learned from his foster parents. Only a male that has mastered these latter songs has a chance to be accepted by a female.

Just how perfectly whydahs learn the songs of exotic finches is demonstrated by the following experiment: If a tape of a whydah singing the song of its brood host is played to the right species of exotic finches, these will immediately try to establish contact with their supposed fellows by responding with songs of their own. Dr. J. Nicolai from Germany and Dr. R. Payne from the United States have both studied the brood parasitism of whydahs.

Chapter Eight

Descriptions of Exotic Finches

Exotic finches belong to the family of Estrildidae. They are distributed throughout Africa south of the Sahara, and in Madagascar, southern Asia, New Guinea, Australia, and the Indonesian Islands.

The closest relatives of these small birds (3½ to 5 inches [9–13 cm]) are the African weavers (Ploceidae) and the Fringillidae that are found almost all over the world. From Africa, which is perhaps the original home of the Estrildidae, these finches spread as far as Australia, where completely new species evolved.

A striking feature of exotic finches is the shape of their bills, and fanciers often divide exotic finches into a broad-billed and a thin-billed group. But in a few species it is not altogether clear which category they should be assigned to.

• With a very few exceptions, all so-called *thin-billed* Estrildidae are native to Africa. Birds of this group include the following genera: *Pytilia, Lagonosticta, Uraeginthus, Estrilda, Ortygospiza,* and *Amandava* (India and Indochina).

• The so-called *broad-billed* finches are found in Australia, the Indonesian Islands, and Africa.

• Australia is the home of the Diamond Firetail, the Painted Finch (genus *Emblema*), the Crimson Finch, and the Star Finch (*Neochmia*) (also on New Guinea), the Cherry Finch (*Aidemosyne*), the Bicheno Finch, and the Zebra Finch, and three other species of the genus *Poephila*, and the Gouldian Finch (*Chloebia*).

• The Parrot Finches (genus *Erythrura*) occur not only in Australia but also on the Indonesian Islands.

• The Java Sparrow (*Padda*), the Spice Finch, and the White-backed Munia (both genus *Lonchura*) inhabit only the islands between India and Australia.

• The Pictorella, Chestnut-breasted, and Yellow-rumped Finches of the genus *Lonchura* live in Australia, whereas the Munias (also of the genus *Lonchura*) are found only on smaller islands.

• Broad-billed finches of the genus *Lonchura* (but not *L. malabarica,* which inhabits India and Ceylon), all Mannikins (*Lonchura*), as well as the Cutthroats and the Red-headed

Finch (both of the genus *Amadina*) are found in Africa.

Many species of exotic finches live on steppes with sparse growth of grass, shrubbery, or trees. Very few live in forests and even fewer on high tropical mountains. In recent times a number of species have adapted to living near human settlements and are found in fields and gardens. Some, such as the Zebra Finch and the Crimson Finch, even nest on buildings.

A distinguishing feature of all Estrildidae is that the young birds have striking white, blue, or yellow warts or welts made up of connective tissue at the corners of their mouths, as well as conspicuous markings inside the mouth—dark dots or lines on the roof of the mouth, the tongue, and under the tongue that vary from species to species—that stimulate the feeding instinct in the parent birds.

A few species of exotic finches act as brood hosts to specific kinds of whydahs; they raise a young whydah along with their own offspring. To make this parasitic relationship possible, the baby whydahs not only copy the begging calls and gestures of their foster siblings but also have their hosts' typical markings inside the mouth.

Explanation of Headings

Description: Here you will find the most striking features of the plumage that help identify the species and distinguish it from other similar ones. If the coloration of the male differs from that of the female, this fact is mentioned. The size of the birds is given in inches and centimeters and reflects the length of the fully extended bird from the tip of the bill to the tip of the tail. The smallest species are the Swee Waxbill (3¾ inches [9.5 cm]) and the Goldbreast (3½ to 4 inches [9–10 cm]); the largest are the Pintailed Parrot Finch (6 inches [15 cm]) and the Long-tailed Grassfinch (5¾ inches [14.5 cm]).

Distribution and habitat: Here all regions and countries where the particular species is found are listed. As habitat, the type of landscape the bird lives in is given.

Habits: Under this heading important information about a particular bird's life in the wild is given, especially what kind of surroundings it prefers. Some exotic finches live in trees, some in tall grass, and others on the ground. The ratio of animal protein (insects) to vegetable food (green and ripe seeds) in the diet varies from species to species; different birds have different ways of gathering their food. Also under this heading you will find information on when the mating season normally occurs, the size of a clutch, where nests are built, and what foods the hatchlings are reared on in the wild.

Requirements in captivity: All exotic finches have similar demands for housing, which are discussed in

Chapter Three, Basic Rules for Housing and Care. Here, specific requirements for housing, minimum temperatures, and setting up the aviary or cage are given. If no temperature is mentioned, the species should be kept at 65 to 74°F (18–23°C).

Food: All exotic finches eat green and mature seeds as well as animal proteins. Under this heading, a particular species' favorite kinds of food are mentioned.

Breeding: Different kinds of exotic finches have different requirements for nesting. Some build their nests in dense thickets; others need to be provided with various kinds of nesting boxes. Here you will find what materials your birds need to build nests, their brooding habits, and the kinds of food parents require to rear their young.

Explanation of Specialized Terms

Adult plumage: The feathers of a fully grown, adult bird.

Brood host: Describing one species of bird that incubates the eggs of another species (either along with, or instead of, its own eggs) and raises the young of the parasite species.

Distal face/proximal face: The primary and secondary feathers of the wings and the side feathers of the tail that consist of two asymmetrical halves. The shaft divides the vane into the distal face, which is narrower and stiff, and the proximal face, which is wider and soft.

Down feathers: In adult birds, the down feathers lie underneath the contour feathers and provide warmth. The first plumage of nestlings consists exclusively of down.

Entry hole or passage: A pipelike projection in front of the entry proper of the nest that many exotic finches build.

Harz box: A small nesting box consisting of a wooden frame and wooden bars or grating.

Juvenile molt: The change from the juvenile to the adult plumage.

Juvenile plumage: The first plumage after the down feathers.

Lores, red-lored/gray-lored subspecific groups: Several subspecies of a species that are characterized by either red or gray feathers between the bill and the eyes, such as on the lores.

Molt: The losing of old feathers and replacing them with new ones.

Nestling days: Days a baby bird spends in the nest, starting with the day of hatching and ending when it leaves the nest.

Parasitism: Describing a species of plant or animal that lives off another species.

Preen gland: The gland—also called the uropygial gland—that secretes the fatty substance that keeps the feathers elastic and water-repellent. It is located on the bird's rump, just above the base of the tail.

Roosting nest: A second bowl-shaped nest that many species of exotic finches build on top of their regular round nest. It used to be thought that the male spent the night in this roosting nest during the incubating period. It now seems, however, that roosting nests are meant to fool snakes and distract them from the brood nests.

Important Species

The following list includes more than 50 of the exotic finches most frequently kept by fanciers and in some cases includes notes on some of their less well-known relatives.

An Aurora Finch photographed in the wild.

Aurora Finch
Pytilia phoenicoptera

Description: 4¾ inches (12 cm).

Male: Back, dark ash-gray; shoulders and rump, red-tinged; central tail feathers, crimson; rest of tail, blackish brown with red distal faces; primaries and secondaries and their coverts, gray-brown with red edges; head, gray; belly, gray with undulating horizontal striping.

Female: Duller and more brownish gray; horizontal striping starts at the throat.

Distribution and habitat: Dry savannas from western Africa, Senegal, and Portuguese Guinea to northern Uganda.

Habits: Aurora Finches live in pairs in the northern parts of the Guinea savanna and in dry open forests. They spend most of their time high up in the trees but forage on the ground for grass seeds as well as insects (termites).

Aurora Finches build relatively large but untidy nests at the beginning of the dry period. Fine grass stems and some dry grass form the lining of the nest, with more grass and some flowering heads as a base. A clutch is made up of four fairly large eggs. The diet of the hatchlings probably consists first exclusively of insects; later, green seeds are included.

The Aurora Finch serves as brood host to the Congo Whydah (*Vidua orientalis interjecta*).

Requirements in captivity: These Pytilias need plenty of warmth and should be kept at a room temperature of at least 68°F (20°C).

They also like to bask in the sun. Unlike Melba Finches and Orange-winged Pytilias, this species is quite peaceful and defends only the immediate nesting area during the mating season. These birds do not like to spend much time on the ground and should therefore be given opportunities for perching on bushes and branches in their cage or aviary. If possible, Aurora Finches should be kept in an aviary since they rarely mate in a cage.

Food: Small-grained and hulled millet, some canary and large-grained millet, seeds of grasses and weeds, chickweed, ant pupae, waxmoth larvae, small mealworms. This species usually does not accept egg food.

Breeding: Aurora Finches like to build their nests in thick branches

A Yellow-winged Pytilia resting on a branch.

but will also accept semiopen boxes. They need coconut fibers and stalks of grass and nesting materials as well as lots of feathers to soften the inside of the nest.

To raise the three to four dark-skinned and very downy nestlings, large amounts of animal protein are necessary because otherwise, the parent birds refuse to feed the young and throw them out of the nest. Fresh pupae of small meadow ants, small mealworms, waxmoth larvae, aphids, fly maggots, and spiders make suitable rearing food. In addition, the parents feed the young birds lots of green seeds during their last days in the nest and after they have left it.

Yellow-winged Pytilia
Pytilia hypogrammica

Description: 4¾ inches (12 cm).

Male: Head, brownish gray with crimson red mask extending behind the eyes; back, brownish gray; wings, brown with yellow edges on the feathers; belly, gray; lower belly and sides with undulating horizontal pattern.

Female: Without red on the head; undulating horizontal stripes from throat to tail.

Distribution and habitat: Humid savannas and abandoned farmland in western Africa from Sierra Leone to Lake Chad.

Habits: Yellow-winged Pytilias live in pairs during the mating season and in small flocks at other times. They live on seeds that have dropped to the ground.

Yellow-winged Pytilias and their close relatives, the Aurora Finches, are the only African exotic finches that mate in the dry season. The Yellow-winged Pytilias build three-layered nests in thickets or in dense foliage of low trees. The outside layer consists of blades of grass inside of which are stems and stalks. The innermost layer is made up of flowering heads of grass and some feathers. Both parents sit on the three to four eggs and rear the young together, feeding them insects during the first few days and later adding seeds to their diet.

The Togo Whydah (*Vidua orientalis togoensis*) is the Yellow-winged Pytilia's brood parasite.

Requirements in captivity: Both the Yellow-winged and the closely related Aurora Finch are less sensitive than the Melba Finch, but coming, as they do, from the hot and sunny savannas, they need as much sun as possible and a room temperature of about 68°F (20°C). These birds should ideally be kept in an aviary, especially since they are absolutely peaceful and even during the mating period defend only the immediate nesting area.

Food: Small-grained millet, canary, spike millet, green and sprouted seeds, egg food, ant pupae, and mealworms.

Breeding: Since the early 1970s, these birds have been imported and bred in captivity in increasing numbers, and the species is now kept by many fanciers. Since Yellow-winged Pytilias and Aurora Finches have less stringent demands in the rearing food they require, breeding them in captivity is much easier than breeding Melba Finches. Yellow-winged Pytilias build their nests either in thick branches or in semi-open boxes. Blades of grass and coconut fibers are suitable building materials. The inside of the nest is padded with lots of feathers. Brooding Yellow-winged Pytilias are not disturbed by occasional nest checks. Raising young Yellow-winged Pytilias successfully requires supplying the parents with plenty of animal proteins in the form of ant pupae, finely chopped or freshly hatched mealworms, waxmoth larvae, aphids, and fly maggots. If this kind of rearing food is not available, the parents refuse to feed the nestlings and soon throw them out of the nest.

During their last nestling days and after they have left the nest, the young birds should get lots of green and sprouted seeds. These must always be fresh and as varied as possible.

Orange-winged Pytilia
Pytilia afra

Description: 4¾ inches (12 cm).

Male: Head, gray with bright red mask extending behind the eyes; back and wings, olive-yellow; primaries and secondaries, brown with distal faces orange-yellow; belly, horizontally scalloped with gray; rump and tail feathers, red.

Female: Without red on the head; throat with gray scallop pattern.

Two Orange-winged Pytilias: a female on the left and a male on the right.

Distribution and habitat: Bushy grassland, edge of forests, and open forests in eastern Africa from southern Ethiopia to Mozambique and Angola.

Habits: Orange-winged Pytilias live in pairs in moist grasslands dotted with bushes and like to spend time in the tops of trees, but they forage for food, which consists of grass seeds and probably also of insects, exclusively on the ground.

These birds build their nests in the second half of the rainy season in forked branches of bushes up to 10 feet (3 m) tall. The basic building material is blades and stalks of grass, and the hollow of the nest is padded with some feathers. The two partners help each other incubating

the three to four eggs. The young are fed insects.

Orange-winged Pytilias often act as brood hosts to the Broad-tailed Whydah (*Vidua orientalis*).

Requirements in captivity: Orange-winged Pytilias, like their cousin, the Melba Finch, should not be kept solely in cages. These birds are happy only in a densely planted indoor aviary with access to an outside area. They react badly to changes in temperature and should be kept at 68 to 72°F (20–22°C). The two species differ in their degree of aggressiveness. Orange-winged Pytilias are quite peaceful outside of their mating and rearing periods, but pairs should be isolated when it is time to breed.

Food: Small-grained millet, canary, spike millet, green seeds, sprouted millet, egg food, ant pupae, mealworms.

Breeding: In aviaries, Orange-winged Pytilias build their nests in dense branches or in semiopen boxes. Good building materials are dry grass, bast, coconut fibers, sisal, moss, and, for softness, feathers. These birds are reliable brooders that remain undeterred by nest checks until the young, with their gray down, hatch after 12 to 13 days of incubation. If the parent birds are not given the right rearing food at this point, they throw the hatchlings out of the nest. They have to have ant pupae of various sorts and plenty of green seeds. They will not take waxmoth larvae, which Melba Finches eat with relish. As the fledglings get ready to leave the nest, the parents feed them more and more seeds.

After the juvenile molt, young Orange-winged Pytilias about three months old develop some variations in coloration. Some birds have a more brownish and others a gray plumage. This difference is no indication of sex.

Melba Finch
Pytilia melba

Description: 4¾ to 5¼ inches (12–13.5 cm).

Male: Head, gray with red mask; back, olive green; crop area, yellow or olive yellow; belly, horizontally striped; rump and central tail feathers, dark red. Two subspecific groups exist, the red-lored and the gray-lored.

Female: Like the male, but without the red mask.

Distribution and habitat: Steppes and savannas in tropical Africa.

Habits: Melba Finches live in pairs in the low growth of thornbush steppes and seek their food on the ground. They live primarily on grass seeds but also eat insects.

The mating season comes in the second half of the rainy season. Melba Finches generally build their nests in thick bushes or in the low branches of small trees. The basic building material used is grass, and the nest is padded with lots of feathers (mostly of guineafowl). The female lays four to six eggs, and both parents sit on the eggs and feed the young. During the first eight to ten days the young are fed only insects, but later seeds as well.

The gray-lored subspecies serve as brood host to the Paradise Whydah (*Vidua paradisaea*); the red-lored ones, to the Broad-tailed Whydah (*V. orientalis*).

Requirements in captivity: Recently imported birds are difficult to acclimate, but once they have adjusted to the change, they are quite hardy and long-lived. The best setup for them is an indoor aviary with access to a generously planted outdoor aviary, which they can use from May to the end of September. The aviary temperature has to be about 68 to 72°F (20–22°C), and the corners of the aviary have to be densely planted for these birds to breed. Males are aggressive toward each other and toward males of other *Pytilia* species even outside the mating season. Melba Finches therefore have to be kept in single pairs. They will even attack and injure birds that are quite unrelated to them but have red masks—such as the Star Finch. Melba Finches will also not put up with their Orange-winged cousins, and the two species cannot be kept together even in a large aviary that offers plenty of cover. Melba Finches do, however, coexist peacefully with such smaller exotic finches as the firefinches of the genus *Lagonosticta* and the waxbills of the genus *Estrilda*.

Food: Small-grained and hulled millet, canary, spike millet, grass seeds (annual panicled grass), seeds of various weeds; also ant pupae, waxmoth larvae, small, freshly hatched or scalded chopped mealworm larvae, and perhaps egg food.

Breeding: Once Melba Finches have adjusted to their new home they breed quickly. They usually build their nests in thick bushes and sometimes in semiopen boxes or in Harz boxes. They have to be given dry grass and coconut fibers. They are steady brooders and are usually not bothered even if their nests are checked. After 12 to 13 days, the black baby birds, covered with dark

This is a mixed community of exotic finches. A Melba Finch is shown on the extreme left of the perch.

gray fluff, hatch. The fledglings leave the nest at about three weeks and are independent in another two weeks. Unfortunately, most hatchlings in aviaries die during their first few days of life and their bodies are thrown out of the nest by the parents. Adult Melba Finches are, in comparison to most other exotic finches, extremely fussy about the rearing food they offer their young. The baby birds are likely to live only if the keeper is able to offer the parents sufficient quantities of tiny meadow insects and pupae of small meadow ants.

Green Twinspot
Mandingoa nitidula

Description: 4 to 4¼ inches (10–11 cm).

Male: Upper side, a rich olive green; rump and upper tail coverts, tinged orange-red; primaries and secondaries, dark gray-brown with olive gray outer edges; tail, blackish; face, red; throat and upper breast, olive green; belly, black covered with round white spots; eyelids have red rim.

Female: Without red on the head; cheeks and chin, brownish yellow; rump and upper tail coverts, olive green; eyelids have bluish gray rim.

Distribution and habitat: Thickets on the edge of tropical forests, mountain woods, swampy rice fields with nearby bushes from Sierra Leone to southern Ethiopia, northern Angola, Natal, and Transkei.

Habits: Green Twinspots live hidden in low thickets and tall grass where they can quickly find safety from danger. They live on grass seeds and rice, which they pick up off the ground.

The pairs build their nests at the end of the rainy season or early in the dry one in bushes or trees 10 to 16 feet (3–5 m) tall. They use grass as building material. Both partners take turns sitting on the three eggs. The young are reared on insects.

Requirements in captivity: If at all possible, Green Twinspots should have a densely planted aviary with an outside room to live in because they like to dart about among small branches. A single pair can, if necessary, be kept in a large cage that offers enough space for flying with plants that provide plenty of opportunities for climbing and hiding.

Pairs stay together all year, not just during the mating season, and get along peacefully not only with other members of their species but

A Green Twinspot perching on a leafy branch.

also with other exotic finches. Freshly imported birds adjust to an aviary with difficulty at the beginning. They need an even temperature of 68°F (20°C) and a wide range of insect food.

Food: In captivity, Green Twinspots depend heavily on live foods, such as Drosophila larvae, enchytraeids, waxmoth larvae, and flying ants. They also eat small-grained millet, green and sprouted spike millet, and green grass seeds (*Briza media, Agropyrum repens, Dactylis glomerata*).

Breeding: Green Twinspots build their nests either on branches or in a nesting box. They need blades of grass, coconut fibers, bast, pieces of wool yarn, and thin roots, as well as moss and feathers for a soft lining. Like Painted Finches, they use small clumps of earth as a kind of mortar. In captivity, a typical clutch consists of four to five eggs. During the day, the two birds take turns sitting on them; at night both of them sleep in the nest.

The young hatch after 12 or 13 days. Their skin is at first a yellowish flesh color that later turns gray, and they are covered with whitish gray down. If there is any danger near the nest, both the parents and any young ones that are 13 days old or more rattle their bills.

For rearing their young, Green Twinspots need insects in sufficient quantity and variety, as well as all kinds of green seeds. The young birds mature very early. One pair of siblings built a nest at ten weeks of age, and the female laid fertile eggs.

Peter's Twinspot
Hypargos niveoguttatus

Description: 4¾ to 5¼ inches (12–13.5 cm).

Male: Crown and neck, olive gray; back and wings, cinnamon brown; rump and upper tail coverts, red; tail, black; throat, cheeks, and breast, crimson; belly, black with round white spots; eyelids have light blue rim. Five subspecies.

Female: Like the male but with olive gray head; throat, brownish; breast, tinged red.

Distribution and habitat: Dry forests, edges of forests, and bushy gorges in tropical Africa, from Kenya to Mozambique in the east and extending to eastern Zaire and Angola in the west.

Habits: Peter's Twinspots live in pairs in thick, low shrubbery. They collect their food—seeds of grasses

Peter's Twinspots are very colorful birds.

and weeds as well as insects—on the ground.

These birds build their nests in the second half of the rainy season. Grass, plant fibers, and small roots form the basic structure of the nest, which is then padded with some feathers. A clutch consists of three eggs, and the young are fed insects and green seeds.

Requirements in captivity: Newly imported birds have to kept at an even 72 to 77°F (22–25°C), and even later the temperature should not drop below 68°F (20°C) for any length of time.

During the mating season, Peter's Twinspots defend the territory around their nests and go after members of the genera *Pytilia* and *Lagonosticta* quite viciously. If the male enters the mating period before the female does, he also chases her around. You should in any case keep a close eye on these birds and intervene in cases of constant quarreling.

Food: Small-grained millets, canary, sprouted millet, green seeds, ant pupae, waxmoth larvae, egg food, chickweed.

Breeding: Breeding Peter's Twinspots in captivity is usually successful. The birds build their nests on the ground, in all kinds of nesting boxes, or among dense branches. They use blades of grass and coconut fibers as building material and pad the nest with feathers. Birds that were bred in captivity are quite indifferent to occasional nest checks. The young, which are flesh-colored at first and later turn dark, hatch after 12 or 13 days.

As in the case of the Pytilias, it is absolutely crucial that the parents be provided with the proper rearing food, because otherwise they throw the young out of the nest. Give them fresh ant pupae, small insects, spiders, insect larvae, and waxmoth larvae; also include lots of green seeds from the very beginning. Egg food cannot be substituted for insects.

The fledglings leave the nest at the age of three weeks. They are still quite clumsy at this point and sensitive to the cold because they no longer spend the night in the nest. The parents continue to feed them for another two to three weeks, at which time the young become fully independent.

Dybowski's Twinspot
Euschistospiza dybowskii

Description: 4¾ inches (12 cm).

Male: Head, throat, and breast, a dark slate gray; back, shoulders, and rump, crimson; wings, olive brown; belly, black; on the sides, lots of small dots forming horizontal bands; eyelids have purple rims.

Female: Back and rump, a lighter red; belly, slate gray instead of black; rim of eyelids gray.

Distribution and habitat: Rocky regions with grass, riverbanks, and ledges of riverside forests in the savannas of Africa from Sierra Leone to the northeastern Congo and from the western shore of Lake Albert to the southwestern Bahr-el-Ghazal region.

Habits: Dybowski's Twinspots are found mostly on the ground among dense bushes where they search for food. They eat primarily grass seeds and other small seeds but also insects.

Nothing is known as yet about the breeding habits of these birds in the wild.

Requirements in captivity: In recent years these birds have been imported in greater numbers, and they are now successfully bred in captivity. But they do have to be kept in aviaries because they scare easily and react violently in cages. It is best to introduce them into medium-sized aviaries. The behavior of Dybowski's Twinspots resembles that of the firefinches of the genus *Lagonosticta*: They spend a lot of time on the ground, where they eat seeds one at a time. At any sign of danger they disappear into the densest thickets.

A Dybowski's Twinspot enjoying a sunny day in its aviary.

Food: Canary, small-grained millet, sprouted millet, ant pupae, and small mealworms. Dybowski's Twinspots never eat large amounts of any one food, and they like to pick their favorite morsel out of a mixture that should be as varied as possible.

Breeding: Males are very aggressive toward other males of their species during mating time, and they also fight with other birds that have red masks. If a male Dybowski Twinspot is to mate with a strange female, he is moved into her aviary. If the female were moved in with him, he would chase her so mercilessly that no mating would take place and the birds would have to be separated again.

Dybowski's Twinspots often build a base for their nest out of moss in a sheaf of reeds. On top of this base they build a nest out of coconut fibers and dry grass and line it with feathers and hairs. They are quite nervous during brooding and often leave the nest if the nest is checked. They rear their young exclusively on small insects that have to be offered in sufficient amounts.

The difference between the sexes starts to show up after the juvenile molt; the plumage of the males is darker, and the females are gray.

Black-billed Firefinch
Lagonosticta rara

Description: 4¼ inches (11 cm).

Male: Head and back, a dull burgundy red; wings, grayish brown; wing coverts and distal faces of secondaries, tinged burgundy red; breast and sides, dull burgundy and never with white spots; middle of belly, black.

Female: Upper side and head, brownish gray, tinged red; lores, red; breast and sides, gray; middle of belly, black or grayish brown.

Distribution and habitat: Savannas with tall grass and scattered bushes and open acacia forests from Sierra Leone and Nigeria to western Kenya.

Habits: Black-billed Firefinches live in pairs during mating season; otherwise, they form small flocks, sometimes together with Dark Firefinches. They seek their food—small grass seeds and insects—on the ground.

In the second half of the rainy season, Black-billed Firefinches usually build thin-walled nests near to the ground. They choose tufts of tall grass, bushes, piles of brush, or the grass roofs of huts to build on, and use fine stalks and blades of grass and thin roots as building materials. Then the nest is lined with feathers. The three to four baby birds of one hatching are fed primarily small insects.

This species serves as brood host to *Vidua funerea nigeriae.*

Requirements in captivity: Like other *Lagonosticta* species, Balckbilled Firefinches can be kept in large cages, but they will breed only in a thickly planted aviary. There should be thick bushes, shrubs, and tufts of tall grass as well as some open spaces, because these birds

Shown is a male Black-billed Firefinch (left) and a female (right).

like to spend some of their time on the ground. If the temperature drops below 68°F (20°C), Black-billed Firefinches become noticeably less active and quickly catch cold. The temperature should therefore always be somewhat higher for them.

Black-billed Firefinches should be housed with other exotic finches only under careful observation. There are peaceful as well as aggressive individuals of this species, but they get along with species that are smaller than they are.

Food: Small-grained millet, green grass seeds, greens, pupae of meadow ants, aphids, fruit flies.

Breeding: Black-billed Firefinches have been bred successfully in captivity only a few times. The birds usually build their nests in thick tufts of grass, in bushes, or in tall grass on the ground. They need grass, coconut fibers, and feathers as building materials.

The Jos Plateau in Africa is the home of the Bar-breasted Firefinch.

The first week is particularly critical for the survival of the young. If the parent birds do not find enough food to their liking at this time, the feeding instinct ceases to function and the young birds starve. You therefore have to supply as varied a diet as possible of animal proteins: pupae of meadow ants, small insects and spiders, and mealworms. The birds also accept sprouted seeds.

Bar-breasted Firefinch

Lagonosticta rufopicta

Description: 4 inches (10 cm).

Male: Forehead, lores, and sides of head, pink; crown and neck, gray-brown; back, earth brown varying with subspecies; wings, earth brown; tail, blackish with red-tinged distal faces; lower belly and under tail coverts, a pale yellowish brown; belly, a dull pink with many small, dark-rimmed white dots often forming wavy horizontal lines on the breast; upper tail coverts, red.

Female: Like the male but duller shades of color.

Distribution and habitat: Tall grass and brush in the African savannas, especially along riverbanks from Gambia to the southern Sudan and southeastern Uganda.

Habits: Bar-breasted Firefinches live in pairs in savannas, preferably in the brush along rivers but also near farms and towns. As a rule they prefer moister areas than the Red-billed Waxbills. They eat grass seeds for which they forage on the ground.

Like most exotic finches, Bar-breasted Firefinches mate in the second half of the rainy season but sometimes breed as late as one third into the dry season. They build their nests in thick tufts of grass, bushes, or even in creeping plants on the walls of houses. The nests consist of two layers: broad-leafed grasses are on the outside; fine grass panicles line the inside. Feathers provide soft padding. The female lays four eggs, and both parents feed the young on insects.

Bar-breasted Firefinches are brood hosts to whydahs of the species *Vidua wilsoni*.

Requirements in captivity: Freshly imported birds, like many other exotic finches, are very delicate and need plenty of warmth—temperatures of at least 68°F (20°C). They always remain sensitive to wet and cold weather.

Coming from areas with tall grassy vegetation and bushes, these birds need some dense plantings they can take refuge in at any time;

otherwise, they will remain shy and nervous. But they also frequent the open ground, where they search for insects and seeds. An outside aviary should always have an enclosed area where the birds can stay during wet and cold weather. Bar-breasted Firefinches are one of the most aggressive species of exotic finches, and they cannot be housed together with other kinds of exotic finches, even larger ones. A pair that is about to mate should therefore be combined only with quite unrelated, larger birds, such as Fringillidae, parakeets, or small pigeons.

Food: Millet, canary, ant pupae, egg food, waxmoth larvae, spiders.

Breeding: If they are housed and cared for properly, Bar-breasted Firefinches breed quite reliably in captivity. They will build their nests in semiopen or enclosed nesting boxes or in branches. The basic building material used is coarse blades of grass; the inside of the nest is padded with soft grass. Generally, these birds are steady brooders and do not mind nest checks.

Provide sprouted and green seeds, mealworms, large amounts of ant pupae, and other small insects as rearing food.

Once the fledglings leave the nest, the male parent usually takes charge of them and feeds them until they are fully independent.

The closely related Brown Firefinch (*L. nitidula*) is almost identical to its Bar-breasted cousin. It differs from the latter and from all other members of the genus by having grayish brown upper tail coverts. Brown Firefinches prefer moister regions with thick grass and reeds in Angola, Zambia, the southern Congo, and northern Rhodesia. Their requirements for housing and food are the same as those of Bar-breasted Firefinches.

Red-billed Firefinch
Lagonosticta senegala

Description: 4 inches (10 cm).

Male: Head, a rosy crimson that gets gradually less brilliant; tips of feathers, bright red; back of head and neck, crimson mixed with brown in many subspecies; back and wings, brown; rump and upper tail coverts, red; tail, black with crimson rims on the feathers; belly, crimson with tiny white dots on the sides of the breast. Proximal face of the second primary (counting from the outside in) clearly narrows down before the tip (see Jameson's Firefinch). Nine subspecies.

A Red-billed Firefinch feeding one of its offspring.

Female: Upper side, a yellow earth brown to olive brown depending on the subspecies; lighter on the underside. Side of breast often has more white dots than on the male; red spot over the lores.

Distribution and habitat: Dry regions near open waters in Africa from Senegal to Eritrea in the north, to Zululand, Natal, and Cape Province in the Republic of South Africa in the south; also in northern Southwest Africa and southern Angola. Often found near human settlements.

Habits: Red-billed Firefinches live in pairs on dry steppes and scrubland (they favor acacia bushes) alongside rivers. They are also routinely found near villages. They eat small seeds and insects that they pick off the ground.

Red-billed Firefinches mate in the second half of the rainy season as well as early in the dry one, and they build their nest in tufts of grass, small shrubs (close to the ground), under verandas, or in the grass walls inside the huts of African natives. Dry grass is all they need as building material. The inside of the nest is thickly lined with feathers. The female lays three to four eggs, and the nestlings are raised on insects and green seeds.

The Green Indigo-bird (*Vidua chalybeata*) is this species' brood parasite.

Requirements in captivity: All Red-billed Firefinches—but particularly the females—are extremely susceptible to disease if they are recently imported, and they need lots of warmth. Even when they are acclimated, the room temperature should not drop below 65°F (18°C) for any length of time; otherwise, these birds are quite undemanding and are therefore suitable for less experienced bird fanciers. Be sure, however, to buy birds that are already acclimated or were born in captivity. Red-billed Firefinches quickly take to a new aviary since they are also very adaptable when living in the wild. All they need is a rather large open area and some shrubbery. They usually coexist peacefully with others of their kind. Only during the mating season do males occasionally fight.

Food: Small-grained millet, spike millet, green seeds, chickweed, ant pupae, small mealworms, insects.

Breeding: If housed properly, Red-billed Firefinches will usually begin to build nests soon, for which they like to use semiopen nesting boxes or coconut halves. Coconut fibers, bast, sisal, and soft grass can be offered as building material. The inside of the nest is thickly padded with fine hair, wool, and feathers. Occasionally, birds will use old, abandoned nests that they then pad. Red-billed Firefinches are extremely reliable brooders. They feed their young sprouted seeds, egg food, mealworms, enchytraeids, and especially ant pupae. These foods should be offered in sufficient quantity and variety. If live food is lacking, the baby birds starve within the first few days and are thrown out of the nest.

A few days after the first batch of young leave the nest, the female starts laying a new clutch. After a pair has raised three or four sets of young birds, all nesting sites should be removed.

Young Red-billed Firefinches are especially sensitive to the cold and wet after leaving the nest. A heavy dew or a heavy downpour can soak their plumage so severely that they can catch cold and sometimes die. These birds should therefore spend the night in the enclosed part of the aviary during bad weather.

Dark Firefinch

Lagonosticta rubricata

Description: 4¼ inches (11 cm).

Male: Forehead and sides of head, crimson; crown and neck, slate gray, in some subspecies, red or mixed with red; back and wings, olive brown to slate gray; rump and upper tail coverts, a brilliant red; tail, black; throat, breast, belly, and sides, crimson with a few white dots on the breast and upper sides; central area of belly, dark grayish brown to dull black; lower tail coverts, black.

Female: Like the male, but the colors are less brilliant.

Distribution and habitat: Savannas with tall grass interspersed with bushes, edges of forests, low growth in open woods in western, eastern, and southern Africa.

Habits: Dark Firefinches live in the shrubbery of humid areas with lush vegetation. They like to be close to the ground, and they forage for food—small seeds, usually of grasses, and insects—along paths and trails.

Toward the end of the rainy season or early in the dry one the birds build well-concealed nests in bushes, shrubs, or tufts of grass. Big, dry blades of grass are used for the basic construction, and the inside of the nest is lined with soft panicles and feathers. The three to five baby birds are raised by the parents on insects.

The Dusky Indigo-bird (*Vidua funerea*) uses the Dark Firefinches as brood host.

Requirements in captivity: Like all other members of the genus *Lagonosticta*, newly imported Dark Firefinches are especially sensitive and have to be treated with special care—perhaps with a heat lamp—at the beginning. Their need for warmth is great even after the initial period, and they require an even temperature of 68°F (20°C). A well-planted aviary provides the best home for these birds, and they can be observed with ease in such surroundings. Since Dark Firefinches live peacefully with each other and with other kinds of exotic finches, they are good candidates for a mixed flock in an aviary.

Food: Small-grained millet, greens, sprouted millet, live insects, aphids, fresh pupae of meadow ants, small mealworms, Drosophila flies, egg food, and green seeds.

Breeding: Dark Firefinches usually build their nests in very dense brushwood. The nests are made of various grasses and padded with plant silks and feathers. The birds seem quite indifferent to nest checks, but if they sense any danger near the nest, they emit loud warning cries for a long time.

The dark gray hatchlings are fed exclusively animal foods at first—pupae of meadow ants, Drosophila flies, egg food, small mealworms, aphids—which are supplemented from the tenth day on with green and sprouted seeds. There should always be sufficient quantities of fresh food available to ensure the survival of the young birds. After leaving the nest, the young are fed primarily by the male parent.

Very similar to the Dark Firefinch—and in the past considered a subspecies of *L. rubricata*—is the Kulikoro Firefinch (*L. virata*), which is found exclusively in the rocky hills (koppjes) between Bamako and Mopti (Mali). This bird differs so much in song and behavior from the

Dark Firefinch that it has to be regarded as a separate species. Its requirements in captivity are the same as those for the Dark Firefinch.

Jameson's Firefinch
Lagonosticta rhodopareia

Description: 4¼ inches (11 cm).

Male: Forehead, lores, and above the eyes, vivid pink; crown and neck, brownish gray to brown; back and wings, fawn brown; rump and upper tail coverts, red; tail, black; sides of head and belly, red with white dots on the breast and upper sides of body. In contrast to the Red-billed Firefinch, the proximal face of the secondary primary (counting from the outside in) does not narrow before the tip.

Female: Crown, neck, and sides of head, brownish gray, sometimes with a red tinge.

Distribution and habitat: Bushes along riverbanks in thorn forests; also open dry forests in eastern Africa from Eritrea to Transvaal; Angola, Zaire estuary.

Habits: Jameson's Firefinches always live in pairs and are found in the brush along riverbeds or in sparse forests. They are the equivalent of the Dark Firefinches in these arid regions. Their food consists of small seeds—mostly of grasses—as well as insects that they find on the ground.

The pairs build nests close to the ground toward the end of the rainy season or shortly thereafter. Usually they choose small bushes or thick grass to nest in, and they make do

Two Jameson's Firefinches: a female (left) and a male (right).

with coarse dry grass as building material. The inside of the nest is lined with finer grass and feathers. The female lays three to five eggs. The young are fed insects.

Jameson's Firefinches are brood hosts to *Vidua funerea*.

Requirements in captivity: Newly imported birds should be acclimated between 68 and 77°F (20–25°C). Later they become somewhat hardier but still crave sun and heat and must have a place to get warm even during the summer. They do best in an inside aviary with an outside flight. The aviary should be planted with thick bushes and tufts of tall grass that offer the birds cover and nesting sites.

Food: Small-grained millet, green and sprouted seeds, pupae of meadow ants, small mealworms, egg food, and—for variety—waxmoth larvae.

Breeding: So far, very few Jameson's Firefinches have raised young in captivity. The main key to success is a varied animal food diet and an aviary with plenty of opportunity for hiding. Jameson's Firefinches build their nests close to the ground in thick brush. They need dry grass, coconut fibers, moss, and lots of feathers. The incubation period is 12 days. The hatchlings have dark skin and gray down. It is crucial that the parent birds be offered plenty of live foods, particularly ant pupae, to rear their young on. The baby birds stay in the nest for only 17 days and then move into low thickets but still appear on the ground to be fed.

A Masked Firefinch sitting on a broad leaf in a grassy area.

When they start feeding themselves, they pick the food off the ground, so the food should therefore be sprinkled there.

The plumage of the young males has a rosy sheen to it soon after the fledglings leave the nest, whereas the females are all brown.

Masked Firefinch
Lagonosticta larvata

Description: 4¼ inches (11 cm).

Male: Edge of forehead, sides of head, and throat, black; crown, gray; back and wings, grayish wine color; primaries and secondaries, dark grayish brown; belly, pale wine red with white dots on the sides of the breast; tail, black; central tail feathers, a dark red.

Female: head, yellowish gray without any black; upper side, brownish with a wine-red tinge; belly, yellowish gray.

Distribution and habitat: Bamboo stands, bush savannas, tall grass in open forests from Gambia,

Senegal, and Portuguese Guinea to southwestern Sudan, Zaire, and northern Uganda.

Habits: Masked Firefinches live in pairs and are usually found in tall, thick grass. They pick their food (primarily grass seeds, but also insects) off the ground.

The birds build their nests during the rainy season in small bushes, piles of brush, and in open farmland. The nests are loosely constructed out of grass, and the interiors lined with fine panicles and feathers. A clutch consists of four eggs, and both parents feed the baby birds insects.

This species serves as brood host to the *Vidua funerea nigeriae.*

Requirements in captivity: While settling in, these cold-sensitive birds need relatively high, constant temperatures (72 to 77°F [22–25°C]). Later, they still need a minimum temperature of 65 to 68°F (18–20°C). If they live in an outdoor aviary, they have to have access to a heated room where they can warm up. Masked Firefinches are absolutely compatible with other members of their species as well as with other exotic finches. To breed successfully, pairs of Masked Firefinches usually have to be kept in an aviary.

Food: Small-grained millets, spike millet, sprouted millet, green seeds of grasses and other plants; also, lots of insects, such as small ants, fresh ant pupae (if possible of various meadow ants), small mealworms, waxmoth larvae, fruit flies, and some egg food.

Breeding: Soon after settling in, Masked Firefinches often begin building a nest in a bush or tucked away in some grass, reeds, or heather. They need soft stalks of grass, bast, or coconut fibers for building and line the nest with a tight layer of hair and feathers.

After an incubation period of 11 to 12 days, the very dark baby birds hatch. They have few down feathers. If the proper rearing food is not available, they are thrown out of the nest. It is therefore essential to have fresh ant pupae, small mealworms, waxmoth pupae, fruit flies, and if possible other small insects on hand for them.

After leaving the nest, the young birds should spend a few days in a protected room so that they will not suffer harm from cold and rain.

Red-cheeked Cordon-bleu
Uraeginthus bengalus

Description: 4¾ inches (12 cm).

Male: Upper side, brown, varying depending on the subspecies from grayish brown to fawn color; sides of head, breast, sides, light blue; a longish bright red patch in auricular region; middle of lower body and under tail coverts, a light red grayish brown; tail, dark blue; upper tail coverts, light blue.

Female: Without the red patch in the auricular region; blue areas less bright and smaller and in some races brownish.

Distribution and habitat: Steppes and savannas, dry forests, hedges outside of villages in tropical Africa from Senegal and Guinea south as far as Tanzania, southeastern Zaire, and eastern Angola.

Habits: Cordon-bleus always live in pairs and are found in thornbushes. They seek their food—small seeds, primarily of grasses, as well as termites and other insects—on the ground.

These birds build their nests during the rainy season or shortly after in thick thornbushes or thorn trees. They use stalks of grass with seeds in racemes or panicles for building the nest and line it with loose panicles and sometimes with feathers. Sometimes they also use abandoned weavers' nests or build nests near wasps' nests. The female usually lays four to five eggs. The young are raised on insects.

Requirements in captivity: Cordon-bleus are among the most popular exotic finches, but they are very delicate. Freshly imported birds have to be acclimated with special care and be exposed to a heat lamp at the beginning. If they are moved to an aviary later, you have to check to see that they find their way around in their new surroundings. These birds always remain cold-sensitive, and the nighttime temperature should never drop below 65°F (18°C), because they sleep perched on a branch rather than sitting in a nest; otherwise, Cordon-bleus have no special requirements for housing— they can be kept either in a spacious flight cage or an aviary. But during mating period no more than one pair should be kept together because the

Red-cheeked Cordon-bleus fit in well in mixed finch communities.

males are often very aggressive toward each other.

Food: Small-grained millet, green and sprouted seeds, greens.

Breeding: Cordon-bleus are as a rule good and reliable breeders, and the pairs stay together all year. They like to build their nests in thick bushes, piles of brush, or conifers, and will use coconut fibers, bast, grasses, and feathers as building materials. They should be left alone during the 12-day incubation period because they almost always leave the nest if disturbed. During the first few days after hatching, the young birds need lots of live food such as ant pupae, daphnia, fly larvae, aphids, and water fleas. From the second week on, they also eat green seeds. If the proper food is not available, they starve and are thrown out of the nest.

When the young birds, at about 21 days, leave the nest, they are

The Violet-eared Waxbill has a striking plumage.

extremely sensitive to cold and wetness. The breeder has to watch over them carefully during this period and keep them indoors at night and during bad weather.

The male of the Angolan Cordon-bleu (*U. angolensis*), 4¾ inches (12 cm), can be distinguished from his Red-cheeked cousin right away because he lacks the red patch in the auricular region. This species lives in pairs in the dry thornbush steppes from Zaire to Rhodesia and Tanzania.

The male Blue-headed Cordon-bleu (*U. cyanocephala*), 5½ inches (14 cm), is distinguished by his bright blue crown, and the female has a blue forehead. This species inhabits the dry steppes and semi-deserts of eastern Africa.

All three species of Cordon-bleus are very closely related to one another. Their habits, breeding, diet, and requirements in captivity are practically identical.

Violet-eared Waxbill
Uraeginthus granatina

Description: 5½ inches (14 cm).

Male: Body, chestnut brown; band across forehead, cobalt blue; cheek patch, deep violet; throat, black; rump, blue.

Female: Body, light brown; band across forehead, narrower and paler than in the male; cheek patch, light violet; throat, light brown.

Distribution and habitat: Dry thornbush steppes and open acacia woods with low growth in southern Africa from southern Angola to northern Rhodesia and from southwest Africa to southern Rhodesia.

Habits: Violet-eared Waxbills live in pairs and forage for food—insects and small seeds—only on the ground.

These birds breed late in the rainy season or early in the dry season. Their roundish nests are built in thornbushes and lined with feathers. Both parents take turns sitting on the three to five eggs. Every time the male comes to relieve the female, he carries a feather to the nest. The young birds are raised on insects.

Violet-eared Waxbills serve as brood hosts to the Shaft-tailed Whydah (*Vidua regia*).

Requirements in captivity: Violet-eared Waxbills are especially dependent on warmth, and during the initial adjustment period they should be housed in a large cage that is warmed with a heat lamp (100 watt infrared bulb). It is inadvisable to keep them exclusively in a cage or indoor aviary because they need a lot of direct, unfiltered sunlight.

They are really comfortable only in an outdoor aviary with access to an enclosed room with temperatures ranging from 68 to 77°F (20–25°C).

Violet-eared Waxbills get along only with their mates. They will not put up with closely related species such as the Purple Grenadier.

Food: Small insects; spiders; small, freshly hatched or scalded and chopped mealworms, waxmoth larvae, ant pupae, and especially egg food; small-grained and spike millet fed dry or sprouted; half-ripe, homegrown millet ears; plenty of chickweed; half-ripe grass seeds (such as annual bluegrass); half-ripe heads of dandelion and sow thistle seeds.

Violet-eared Waxbills require a diet rich in animal proteins. If they are fed only seeds, they will inevitably come down with intestinal disorders and die.

Breeding: If provided with adequate housing, Violet-eared Waxbills will get ready to breed in the spring after their first molt. The male builds the nest in thick bushes (yew and boxwood) preferably using coconut fibers, dry grass, and lots of feathers. But he will also accept a closed box with a semiopen front as a nesting site. Both parent birds are steady sitters. The blackish young with just a few white downy feathers hatch after 13 days. At this time the keeper has to provide an especially nutritious diet of ant pupae, waxmoth larvae, and small spiders and mealworms; otherwise, the hatchlings will starve.

Many Violet-eared Waxbills sit on the nestlings only the first five nights, which is probably enough in their native habitat but falls short of what is needed in our latitudes and leads to the young birds' death. If your birds follow this pattern, the hatchlings should be moved to a well-heated room in the evening in a thickly padded box and returned to their nest in the morning before the parent birds resume feeding. If you delay too long in returning the nestlings in the morning, the parents will no longer accept them. After the young birds leave the nest the whole family should be locked indoors for the first few nights until the young birds settle in the room on their own at dusk.

Between the 24th and 35th day, the young birds molt those parts of the head plumage that are violet, blue, and black in the adult male. At this time the pairs start forming their permanent bonds.

Purple Grenadier
Uraeginthus ianthinogaster

Description: 5¼ inches (13.5 cm).

Male: Body, reddish brown; line over lores, ring around the eye, and cheek, violet-blue; belly, reddish brown more or less maculated with blue.

Female: Basically light brown; feathers on breast and sides with white bars; ring around the eye, whitish or bluish.

Distribution and habitat: Dry thornbush steppes in eastern Africa from southern Abyssinia and Somalia to southern Tanzania (Iringa).

Habits: Purple Grenadiers live in pairs, usually in bushes or tall grass. They forage for their food—grass and other small seeds and, probably, insects as well—on the ground.

These birds breed during the rainy season. They build their spherical nests in low bushes. The male continues to pad the nest with feathers during the incubation period. Both parents sit on the four to five eggs, the male usually during the day and the female at night.

Purple Grenadiers serve as brood hosts to the Straw-tailed Whydah (*Vidua fischeri*).

Requirements in captivity: Newly imported birds are extremely sensitive, need lots of warmth, and have to be treated with special care at the beginning. Coming from the open thornbush steppes, they need a lot of sun and should be housed in a well-planted outdoor aviary with access to a closed room where the temperature ranges around 72 to 79°F (22–26°C) and never dips below 65°F (18°C) at night.

Purple Grenadiers generally live in peace with other exotic finches and are therefore good candidates for a mixed community. But they are sometimes belligerent toward closely related species, such as the Cordon-bleus, and it is therefore wise to proceed with caution when bringing these two kinds of birds together.

Food: Small-grained and spike millet, sprouted millet, small waxmoth larvae, ant pupae, enchytraeids, egg food, green seeds, greens, perhaps scalded mealworms.

Breeding: Purple Grenadiers build their nests out of dry grass and coconut fibers in bushes and take turns sitting on the eggs. After 12 to 14 days, the brownish, almost naked young hatch. To raise the brood, the parent birds have to be given a very nutritious diet of live foods, such as pupae of small meadow ants, small flies, spiders, fruit flies, daphnias, and copepods.

The hatchlings open their eyes after eight days, and after two to three weeks the young birds leave the nest but return at night for another week or two to sleep in the old nest.

The young birds are still not fully independent when, at about 35 days of age, they start molting the feathers on the head that are blue in adult males. From then on, they have the sex-specific coloration of adult birds, and pairs establish their permanent bonds.

A Purple Grenadier rests on a perch in an aviary.

Lavender Waxbill

Estrilda caerulescens

Description: 4¼ inches (11 cm).

Male and female: rump, upper and under tail coverts, and central tail feathers, bright crimson; short, dark eyeline; rest of plumage a delicate blue-gray that is lightest at the cheeks and throat and darker on the belly.

Distribution and habitat: Grassland dotted with bushes, short grass along thickets, thornbushes among rocks in western Africa from Senegal and Gambia to Cameroon and the Shari region.

Habits: Lavender Waxbills are gregarious birds that live in small flocks on the ground as well as in bushes, where they hunt for insects and pick grass seeds from racemes and panicles.

Pairs of Lavender Waxbills build their nests in the second half of the rainy season in forked branches of bushes and trees. The nest is of grass and has an entry passage. The female lays four eggs. Both partners sit on the eggs and raise the young, feeding them primarily insects.

Requirements in captivity: Freshly imported birds in particular need plenty of warmth and should be kept at around 77°F (25°C) for the first few weeks after the move from their native habitat. Lavender Waxbills get along peacefully with other species but males sometimes fight with males of the same species during the mating season. Pairs should therefore be kept separately if you wish to raise baby birds. Lavender

A typical Lavender Waxbill in the wild.

Waxbills are almost constantly in motion and should be kept in an indoor aviary with access to an outside area. If kept in cages, they have to be given a chance to fly freely in the room to satisfy their need for moving. Lavender Waxbills are nest sleepers and spend the night in unused nests of other exotic finches or weavers.

Food: Lavender Waxbills need relatively large amounts of animal proteins such as small, scalded mealworms, fresh ant pupae, waxmoth larvae, small spiders, and insects. This diet is to be supplemented with small-grained and spike millets, green, homegrown ears of millet, plenty of chickweed, green grass seeds (annual bluegrass), and heads of dandelions and sow thistles.

Breeding: As soon as a male and a female have gotten used to each other, they will start to breed. They build their nests either in thick bushes or in semiopen nesting

A Swee Waxbill huddling in some tall grass.

boxes or Harz boxes. Long grasses and coconut fibers are needed as building materials. The entry hole is at the bottom of the nest. Occasionally they will accept weavers' nests to breed in. Both partners are steady brooders, but sometimes even a single nest check may drive them off the nest. The young hatch after 15 days. The parent birds will feed their young adequately only if they get a proper rearing diet of fresh pupae of meadow ants, waxmoth larvae, aphids, daphnia, and other small insects and spiders. Later on they will also feed the young green or sprouted millet, grass seeds, and nectar foods.

The young leave the nest as early as 16 to 18 days. The parents continue to feed them for another two weeks until the young get along by themselves.

Swee Waxbill

Estrilda melanotis

Description: 3¾ inches (9.5 cm).

Male: Crown and nape, dark bluish gray; back and wings, yellowish brown to olive green with fine dark crossbarring; rump, red; tail, black; lores, side of head, and throat, black or light gray, depending on race; crop and sides of neck, whitish; breast, blue-gray; sides of body, yellowish gray; belly, dull ocher yellow. Four subspecies.

Female: No black on the head; sides of head, whitish; rump, often a yellowish red; lower body, more gray and less ocher yellow.

Distribution and habitat: Edge of mountain woods, clearings, shrubbery, hedges, and gardens in southern and eastern South Africa, Angola, southwestern Zaire, eastern Africa, Ethiopia, and southeastern Sudan.

Habits: Pairs stay together only during the breeding period; otherwise, Swee Waxbills live in flocks. They live on grass seeds, which they find on the ground or pick out of seed heads.

Swee Waxbills build their roundish nests during the rainy season in bushes or small trees, or they may adopt abandoned weavers' nests. They need stalks of grass for building, but they fit them together only loosely. The hollow of the nest is lined with grass racemes, plant silks, and feathers. The female lays four to six eggs, and the young birds are raised primarily on insects.

Requirements in captivity: Swee Waxbills are among the most peaceful exotic finches and become quite friendly toward people. Sometimes they can even be hand-fed. They can exist comfortably in a large cage with some dense branches, but they are unlikely to breed there. If you keep them in an aviary, you should remember that these birds do not like to spend much time on the ground. You should therefore place their food on a raised surface. The lower temperature limit for Swee Waxbills is 63 to 65°F (17–18°C).

Food: Small-grained millets (both dry and sprouted), spike millet, green millet seed, sow thistle and dandelion seeds, fresh pupae of meadow ant, enchytraeids, and small insects.

Breeding: Swee Waxbills usually build nests out of grasses and coconut fibers in bushes or climbing vines. The hollow is padded with feathers or cotton wool. No matter how trusting they may be at other times toward people, they will abandon the nest at the slightest disturbance during brooding. The young birds have long, light-colored downy feathers. To ensure their survival, you have to supply small insects—ant pupae, aphids, and enchytraeids—some of which the parent birds like to catch themselves in the aviary. When the young birds can manage on their own, they should be moved out of the breeding aviary because they like to continue sleeping in their old nest and will get in the way of a new brood.

Orange-cheeked Waxbill
Estrilda melpoda
Description: 4 inches (10 cm).

This photograph shows why Orange-cheeked Waxbills acquired their name.

Male and female: Crown, dark bluish ash gray; back and wings, fawn-colored; rump, red; tail, black; around the eyes and sides of head, yellowish to reddish orange; belly, light bluish ash gray; middle of belly, yellow ocher. Three subspecies.

Distribution and habitat: Tall grass of savannas and along water, swamps, on the edge of farmland in western Africa from Senegal, Gambia, Cameroon, and northern Zaire to the western shore of Lake Albert; southward from Cameroon to northern Angola and across Katanga to northern Rhodesia.

Habits: Orange-cheeked Waxbills live in small flocks. They do not usually form large swarms like the Common Waxbills. During the mating season, which coincides with the rainy season, Orange-cheeked Waxbills are always found in pairs.

The nests are tucked away and hidden between other plants in thick grass or occasionally in low bushes.

Often there is a roosting nest on top. Stalks and blades of grass and seed heads are used as basic building material as well as for lining the inside. The female lays five to six eggs, and both parents feed the young with insects. When breeding time is over, Orange-cheeked Waxbills live exclusively on grass seeds that they pick out of the seed heads or—more rarely—gather on the ground.

Requirements in captivity: Orange-cheeked Waxbills are among the most commonly imported African finches. They are relatively undemanding and are therefore suitable for beginners. A pair can be housed in a large flight cage (3-feet [1-m] long) or in an aviary.

At mating time some pairs become aggressive and may disturb other breeding birds. Such troublemakers have to be removed from the aviary.

Food: Small-grained and spike millets, green seeds, lettuce seeds, ant pupae, aphids, Drosophila.

Breeding: Since Orange-cheeked Waxbills always remain somewhat timid, it is especially important to provide well-protected nesting sites for breeding. The birds usually build their nests in hidden spots under tufts of grass or close to the ground in thickets. Like their relatives, the Black-rumped Waxbills, they like to decorate the nest, which is built out of coconut fibers and grass stalks, with white objects. Avoid nest checks during the incubation period, or the birds will usually abandon their eggs.

Like all other members of the genus *Estrilda*, Orange-cheeked Waxbills have to have live insects and pupae of small meadow and lawn ants to feed to their young because they generally reject egg food and similar foods.

Black-rumped Waxbill
Estrilda troglodytes

Description: 4 inches (10 cm).

Male: Crown, back, and wings, light brownish gray, closely barred; lores and strip across the eyes, red; upper tail coverts and tail, black; sides of head and belly, a light, brownish ash gray with a slight pink cast to it; sides, finely barred.

Female: Like the male but the pink on the belly is fainter.

Distribution and habitat: Dry steppes in northern tropical Africa from Senegal and Gambia in the west all the way to northwestern Ethiopia and southern and western Eritrea in the east and from the Sudan down to northwestern Uganda; also southwestern Saudi Arabia.

Habits: Black-rumped Waxbills like to inhabit the brush along rivers that run during the rainy season and the bushes of open grasslands, where they live primarily on seeds.

In the second half of the rainy season they build their nests either right on the ground or in the base of bushes. Often they build a semicovered roosting nest on top of the pile of nesting materials that contains the regular nest. The three to six young are raised primarily on insects.

Requirements in captivity: Black-rumped Waxbills can be kept in large flight cages at least 3 feet (1 m) long or in well-planted aviaries with as much flying space as possible. They generally coexist peacefully with others of their own kind as well as with other species even during the mating period as long as enough nesting sites are provided. Once they have weathered the initial acclimating period, Black-rumped Waxbills are quite hardy and can stand temperatures with a lower limit of 59°F (15°C).

Food: Small-grained and spike millets, lots of green grass seeds, weed and lettuce seeds, pupae of meadow ants, aphids, Drosophila.

Breeding: Black-rumped Waxbills breed quite readily in well-planted aviaries. They build their nests well camouflaged by thick bushes on the ground and are reluctant to make use of nesting boxes. Fine grass, bast, and coconut fibers are used as building materials, and the interior of the nest is lined with feathers and plant silks and sometimes decorated with striking white objects. A clutch consists of three to six eggs. The pink baby birds, covered with bluish down, hatch after 11 to 12 days, and the parent birds raise them without complications if they are given enough ant pupae, aphids, Drosophila, soaked spike millet, and green seeds. The fledglings leave the nest after three weeks but return to it at night for some time.

The closely related Rosy-rumped Waxbill (*E. rhodopyga*), 4¼ inches

A Black-rumped Waxbill grasping a blade of grass.

(11 cm), is somewhat darker than its Black-rumped cousin and has red instead of black upper tail coverts, a black bill, and dark red lores that extend across the eyes. It inhabits the dry grasslands and thick scrub along rivers in eastern Africa. The requirements for housing, breeding, and feeding are the same as for the Black-rumped Waxbill.

Common Waxbill
Estrilda astrild

Description: 4½ inches (11.5 cm).

Male: Upper side is grayish to fawn-colored (the shade varies with different subspecies). Except on the primaries, it has fine, wavy, horizontal lines that are thinnest at the crown. A bright red stripe extends from the bill past the eyes; sides of head and throat, whitish brown-gray to white (depending on the race); the throat, often with a slight pink tinge; belly, a pale brownish gray with dark, wavy, horizontal lines; depending on

The Common Waxbill is found in the tropical and southern regions of Africa.

the subspecies, the lower body has a more or less pink cast.

Female: Similar to the male, but paler on the upper side; the pink on the lower body is fainter and less extensive.

Distribution and habitat: Marshy areas, tree growths along rivers in steppes and savannas, tall grass, near rivers with tall grass and scrub, gardens, sugar cane plantations in tropical and southern Africa.

Habits: Common Waxbills live primarily on grass seeds that they pick off the ground and out of the seed heads, but they also eat insects. They live together in pairs during the breeding season.

Common Waxbills build their nests during the rainy season in hedges, trees, and climbing vines. They need stalks of grass as nesting material as well as for the base of the roosting nest that they construct above the regular nest. The inside of the nest is lined with blades of grass and feathers. The brood of four to six young is raised on insects.

This species serves as brood host to the Pintailed Whydah (*Vidua macroura*).

Requirements in captivity: Freshly imported birds are quite delicate and must be acclimated with care. Later they become quite hardy and do well as long as the temperature is above 59°F (15°C). If at all possible, the birds should be kept in an aviary because they hardly ever breed in a cage. Common Waxbills make good members of a mixed community of exotic finches because they defend only the immediate surroundings of their nests. They should be provided with plenty of dense bushes where they can dart about and build their nests.

Food: Small-grained and spike millets, green and sprouted seeds.

Breeding: Common Waxbills usually build their nests in thick bushes about 1½ to 5 feet (50–150 cm) off the ground. They need fine grasses and coconut and bast fibers as building materials. For lining the nest, they prefer plant silks, hairs, and feathers. The round nests are often topped with a bowl-shaped roosting nest. You should refrain from checking the nest during the 11- to 12-day incubation period because these birds are bothered by such disturbances and leave the nest.

To be able to raise their young, the parents have to be given sufficient amounts of live insects and ant pupae, particularly those of small meadow ants.

Black-cheeked Waxbill
Estrilda erythronotos

Description: 5 inches (13 cm).

Male: Crown and back, ash gray with fine dark crossbarring; back, slight crimson tinge; wings, whitish gray with marked black crossbars; rump and upper tail coverts, a vivid crimson; tail, center of belly, and face mask, black; rest of belly, a light ash gray tinged red and in fine wavy lines.

Female: Coloration more subdued; center of belly, blackish gray or gray.

An example of the aptly named Black-cheeked Waxbill.

Distribution and habitat: Dry thornbush steppes of western and interior southern Africa from Tanzania in the north to Iringa in the south and as far west as southwestern Uganda, southern Kenya, and Lake Victoria.

Habits: Black-cheeked Waxbills live in pairs in dry thornscrub. They often perch on low branches and pick the seeds from the top of grasses above them. During the breeding period they also eat small insects. They are also often observed sitting high up in acacia trees carefully picking the flowers apart, presumably to get at the nectar inside them. They often spend the night in abandoned weavers' nests.

Black-cheeked Waxbills build their nests in the second half of the rainy season, usually in trees. The enclosed nests with entry holes are built of grass stalks and seed heads and often have a small roosting nest above them.

The three to four hatchlings of a clutch are raised on insects.

In eastern Africa, the Black-cheeked Waxbill is used as a brood host by the Steel-blue Whydah (*Vidua hypocherina*).

Requirements in captivity: Black-cheeked Waxbills live in the hot thornscrub of Africa, as do the Violet-eared Waxbills, and the two species need similar quarters. Freshly imported birds need heat lamps at the beginning. Later they should live in an outdoor aviary with access to a heated room where the temperature should not drop below 68°F (20°C). An occasional cooler sunny summer day does them no harm, but they are very sensitive to wet, cold weather.

Black-cheeked Waxbills get along well with members of their own as well as with other species.

Food: Small-grained and spike millet, ant pupae, mealworms, nectar foods, egg food, sprouted millet, green seeds, aphids, and fruit (apples, oranges cut in half, grapes, pears). They either drink the juice of the fruit or pick out little bits of it.

Breeding: Like most exotic finches, Black-cheeked Waxbills will not breed in a cage but will do so only in an aviary with plenty of shrubbery. They need dry grasses to build their round nests with. The entry hole is below. Breeding ventures usually end in failure because these birds are very fussy about the rearing food they accept. Only if they get animal foods of the right kind—ant pupae and small mealworms—in sufficient quantities will the parents be able to raise their young.

Mr. Andreas of Wilhelmshaven, Germany, has had spectacular success. Under his care, three pairs of imported birds raised their young to adulthood. The parent birds fed their young egg food and mealworms and, above all, grass seeds Mr. Andreas had sowed in saucers and let sprout for three or four days. Some of the birds preferred the tender tips of the sprouts for their young, while others fed them primarily the roots.

Avadavat
Amandava amandava

Description: 4 inches (10 cm).

Male in mating plumage: Lores, black; white stripe below the eye; head, a dark vermilion to scarlet red; back, brown with red-tipped feathers; rump and upper tail coverts, red; wings, dark brown with white spots; tail and middle of belly, black; rest of belly, red with white spots on the sides.

Female: Like the male, but the head is a light brownish gray. Eye stripe goes only as far as the eye. Throat and middle of belly, whitish ocher yellow; sides of body, light brownish gray.

The Avadavat is the only species of exotic finches in which the male has a special mating plumage. The regular male plumage resembles that of the female.

Distribution and habitat: Large parts of India where the climate is not too dry; Burma, southwestern China, Thailand, Indochina, Java, Bali, and most of the Lesser Sunda Islands. Found in reeds, wet areas with tall grass along bodies of water, sugarcane fields, and open brush.

Habits: Outside of mating season, Avadavats often live in large flocks and sometimes nest close together. They live mostly on the ground, where they collect seeds.

Generally, Avadavats breed in the second half of the monsoon season or in the dry season. They build their roundish nests out of grass stalks in thickets or tufts of tall grass. Fine grass and plant silks serve as padding. The female lays four to seven eggs. The presence of lots of insects assures that the young will have plenty to eat.

Requirements in captivity: Part of the aviary or of a flight cage should contain reeds, tall grass, and thick bushes that the birds can dart in and out of and nest in. In the open area they can forage for food and sunbathe. Avadavats need warmth, and an outdoor aviary should always be connected to an enclosed room. In the summer some pairs have been successfully kept in the open where they even mated and raised their young. This was first tried by Jurgen Nicolai in Seewiesen in Upper Bavaria, Germany.

With Avadavats, you have to watch the claws carefully because they often grow too long. If this happens, the birds get caught in the wire mesh and hurt themselves.

During the mating season, these birds should be kept in pairs, at other times in groups. They never bother other kinds of exotic finches.

Food: Small-grained millet, sprouted millet, greens, green seeds, mealworms, ant pupae, aphids, daphnia.

Breeding: In captivity, male Avadavats mate even when in molt or in their unspectacular plumage. Generally these birds are reliable brooders. They usually build their nests in natural sites and need fine grass stalks, hay, bast, and coconut fibers as building materials. The inside of the nest is lined thickly with feathers.

Avadavats are a species of finch that can be kept in a mixed aviary.

After 11 days the dark nestlings hatch and then need lots of ant and mosquito larvae, daphnia, and especially green seeds to eat.

Many pairs keep raising one brood after another, and it is therefore advisable to deprive them of nesting sites no later than after the third clutch so that the birds will not exhaust themselves totally.

In central India the Green Avadavat (*Amandava formosa*), 4¼ inches (11 cm), is found. Its upper side, except for the tail, is olive green. Throat and upper breast are pale yellow; the rest of the underside, a stronger yellow. The sides are olive green with white barring. The colors of the female are more muted. Green Avadavats live in the thick grass along rivers or in farmland. The requirements for housing and food are the same for the two species, and Green Avadavats raise their young just as unproblematically as Avadavats as long as they get ant pupae and live insects.

Goldbreast
Amandava subflava

Description: 3½ to 4 inches (9–10 cm).

Male: Lores, black; eyebrow, rump, and upper tail coverts, red; upper sides of body, greenish gray with pale yellow crossbarring; under tail coverts, orange; rest of belly, bright gold to lemon yellow or, in the northerly subspecies *(A. s. subflava)*, sometimes orange.

Female: Colors more muted than in male; no red stripe over the eye.

A Goldbreast observes its surroundings from a branch.

Distribution and habitat: Wet grassy and reedy wilderness and swampy areas in Africa south of the Sahara except for interior tropical forests and dry regions in southwestern and southern Africa; southwestern Saudi Arabia.

Habits: Except in the mating period, Goldbreasts live together in small groups. They fly to fields and grassy areas in search of food. There they move about on the ground looking for small seeds, mostly of grasses, and small insects.

Mating time for these birds comes at the end of the rainy or the beginning of the dry season. The northern subspecies (*A. s. subflava*) builds nests in the grass among tall stalks or in small bushes. The nest is made up of fine grasses and is lined with seed heads and feathers. The southern subspecies (*A. s. clarkei*) usually takes over abandoned round nests of other species and adds some more feathers as padding. A clutch consists of four to five eggs. During the first week, the hatchlings need small insects to eat, later green grass seeds.

Requirements in captivity: Goldbreasts are some of the hardiest exotic finches. Still, freshly imported birds are delicate and have to be acclimated with care. During mating season the males fight energetically, and Goldbreasts should therefore be kept in single pairs. They get along peacefully with other species.

Food: Small-grained millets, green seeds, sprouted millet, ant pupae, small mealworms, and small insects.

Breeding: Soon after having adjusted to their new home, Goldbreasts are likely to start building nests at various heights in thick bushes. They will also accept closed or semiopen nesting boxes, or they may move into abandoned nests of other species. Some nests are built crudely while others are carefully constructed out of hay, bast, and coconut fibers.

The hatchlings, which are covered with white down, make their appearance after 11 days. To raise them successfully, the parent birds need pupae of small meadow ants, small insects, or mealworms. Later, the young receive green seeds as well.

Quail Finch

Ortygospiza atricollis
Description: 4 inches (10 cm).

Male: Forehead and lores, black; eye region and chin, black in the subspecies that was first described and that gave the species its Latin name (*O. a. atricollis*); other subspecies have white rings around the eyes; upper side, gray-brown; upper breast and sides have either narrow crossbars or wide ones that are white with blackish edges against a gray-brown ground; lower breast, reddish brown.

Female: head and throat, brown-gray without any black; crossbarring less bold, and colors generally more muted.

Distribution and habitat: Open grasslands from South Africa across Rhodesia up to the southern Sudan; highlands from Ethiopia to Eritrea; and in western Africa from Lake Chad and eastern Nigeria to Liberia.

Habits: Quail Finches spend all their time on the ground, where they find their food. They not only hop from place to place but also run along the ground like quail. The long back toe is much less curled than it is in exotic finches that live in trees—an obvious sign of adaptation to ground dwelling.

Late in the rainy or early in the dry season, Quail Finches build their well-distinguished nests on the ground out of dry, earth-colored leaves. The inside of the nest is lined with fine grass stalks, soft seed heads, and feathers. Both parents sit on the four to six eggs, and grass seeds have to be provided for rearing the young.

Requirements in captivity: Since Quail Finches live almost exclusively on the ground, their needs differ from those of other exotic finches. Cages are not suitable for them because there is not enough floor area to run around on. If these birds have to be housed temporarily in a cage for some reason, a cloth should be stretched across the top. Otherwise, birds can hurt themselves badly if they fly up suddenly. If you have an aviary, it should be at least 5 feet (1.5 m) high, and it also should have a cloth stretched across the top. Just as important is that the bottom be planted in dense grass and reeds. In addition, these birds need a soft surface made of moss, hay, or some cloth to rest and sleep on at night. The aviary also has to have a sufficiently large open area, because Quail Finches like to take some longer flights. The birds do not do well in temperatures below 66°F (19°C), and a single exposure to a downpour can cause a potentially fatal cold. Any outdoor aviary should therefore be connected to an enclosed room that the birds can retreat to in bad weather. Since birds of this species are absolutely peaceful toward each other as well as toward other exotic finches, several pairs can be kept together without problems.

Food: Small-grained millets, spike millet, greens, ant pupae, daphnia, and various insects.

Breeding: Like Diamond Firetails, Quail Finches are extremely choosy about picking a mate and will often completely ignore a partner that is foisted on them. They have to be given the chance to pick their partner out of a group. Their round nests are built on the ground out of dry grass, coconut fibers, and many feathers. Nest checks are strictly forbidden. During their first few days, the hatchlings are fed only insects of various sorts; later they are given green and sprouted seeds as well.

Painted Finch
Emblema picta

Description: 4¼ inches (11 cm).

Male: Forehead, rump, and upper tail coverts, scarlet; upper side, brown; lores, cheeks, chin, and upper throat, scarlet; sides of head, brown; belly, black with round white dots; red stripe down the breast; upper mandible, black; lower one, red.

Female: Red only on lores and around the eyes; colors on belly paler and with more white dots.

Distribution and habitat: Dry, rocky grassland along rocky mountain ranges in northern and northwestern Australia, western Queensland, and central Australia.

Habits: Painted Finches are found primarily where triodia grass grows along mountain ranges on the steppes of the Australian interior. Only there do they find sufficient water to survive. They are ground dwellers and live on the seeds of various triodia grasses. This species breeds at any time of year whenever there is enough rain to make the grass grow. Then there will be seeds ripening by the time the hatchlings

Like Red-cheeked Cordon-bleus, Painted Finches get along well in mixed finch communities.

have to be fed. The birds nest in the grass close to the ground. The eggs—usually four—are laid in a nest made of green stalks, and the hatchlings are raised on green seeds and probably insects as well.

Requirements in captivity: Painted Finches cannot withstand prolonged cold and wet weather. They need a minimum temperature of 59°F (15°C) and lots of sunshine. In their cage or aviary they should have some dense bushes—broom is best—for nesting as well as largish open areas. Painted Finches never spend the night perched on branches and should therefore have some boards mounted at some distance from the floor; otherwise, they sleep on the ground and easily catch cold. As a rule, Painted Finches get along well with each other as well as

with other exotic finches and lose their shyness toward people.

Food: Small-grained and spike millets, green and soaked seeds, some greens, ant pupae, small mealworms, waxmoth larvae.

Breeding: Painted Finches are fairly easy to raise, but they do have some special requirements. They like to build their nests in natural surroundings and should have dense shrubbery, such as broom or pine branches, available for this purpose. For the base of the nest they need small clumps of earth, stones, bark, and pieces of twigs, and as building materials they like fine, dry pine twigs or other rough-surfaced twigs as well as coconut fibers, grass, plant silks, and feathers.

After 15 to 19 days the young birds hatch, and they have to be fed large quantities of animal foods like fresh ant pupae, small mealworms, and waxmoth larvae, supplemented by fresh greens. If the rearing food offered is not to the parents' liking, they throw the hatchlings out of the nest.

The young birds become independent after three to four weeks. If the parents begin to neglect them before that because they are getting ready to build a nest for a second brood, the whole family should be moved to a cage without nesting sites for a few days.

Diamond Firetail
Emblema guttata

Description: 4¾ inches (12 cm).

Male and female: Lores, black; head, light gray; chin and throat, white; back and wings, deep brown; rump, bright red; tail, black; broad black band across upper breast; sides of body, black with white round spots; belly, white.

Distribution and habitat: Dry, open forests; gardens and other cultivated areas in eastern Australia from southern Queensland to South Australia.

Habits: Outside of the mating season, Diamond Firetails form loose groups of up to 30 birds, and they often breed in colonies. They spend much of their time on the ground, where they forage for grass seeds.

Pairs build their nests of blades and stalks of grass, seed heads, and roots in mistletoe bushes, eucalyptus trees, or acacias. Diamond Firetails also love to nest in the base of aeries. They pad the inside of the nest with plant silks and feathers. A clutch usually consists of five to six eggs. Insects and insect larvae serve as the hatchlings' first food.

Requirements in captivity: Since the Australian ban on exporting exotic finches went into effect in 1960, any birds you can buy were

In the wild, Diamond Firetails are found in Australia.

bred in captivity. Even though they are quite robust, they should have even temperatures of at least 50 to 54°F (10–12°C). Cold and humid weather or soaked feathers can easily lead to possibly fatal colds.

Diamond Firetails should not be kept exclusively in cages because they will either remain shy and wild or get fat. An aviary for them should contain a large open area because they like to dwell on the ground, where they move about in long hops. Birds of this species like to build roosting nests even outside the breeding season and should therefore always have building materials at their disposal. They get along well with other exotic finches and defend their nests only at mating time when they chase other birds—especially closely related Australian species like Long-tailed Grassfinches, Zebra Finches, and Bicheno Finches—sometimes to death.

Food: Small-grained millet, canary, soaked or green spike millet, chickweed, various grass seeds (*Poa annua, Holcus lanatus*), dandelions, sow thistles, fresh ant pupae, mealworms.

Breeding: For Diamond Firetails to produce offspring, they have to be able to pick their own mates out of a fairly large mixed group. Pairs that are brought together by force often refuse to breed for years because they do not like each other.

This species builds huge nests either in thick bushes or on boards or in oversized nesting boxes (7 × 7 × 10 inches [18 × 18 × 25 cm]). They need fresh grass, coconut fibers, sisal, feathers, and shepherd's purse as building materials and should have these available as long as possible. Both partners sit on the eggs and feed the young very conscientiously, but they do have to be given plenty of fresh ant pupae, small or chopped mealworms, aphids, flies, and spiders. The young birds leave the nest after 21 to 25 days and should, as soon as they can manage on their own, be separated from the parents because they can get in the way of later broods. The adult pair should be separated after raising three broods so that they do not get worn out.

Crimson Finch
Neochmia phaeton

Description: 5 inches (13 cm).

Male: Forehead, red; crown, gray-brown; back and wings, brown with a red cast; upper tail coverts, red; mask, throat, breast, and sides, bright red with white dots on sides of breast; under tail coverts and belly are black in the subspecies living in the interior of Australia (*N. p. phaeton*) and white in the subspecies living on the Cape York Peninsula (*N. p. albiventer*) and in New Guinea (*N. p. evangelinae*).

Female: Crown, back, and wings, grayish with red cast; sides of head and throat, pale red; breast and sides of body, brown-gray with white dots on sides of breast; lower body, brownish (*N. p. phaeton*) or white (*N. p. albiventer* and *N. p. evangelinae*).

Distribution and habitat: Along riversides in dry savannas, on

Crimson Finches do not get along with other finches.

coastal plains that are wet year-round in northern Australia (*N. p. phaeton* and *N. p. albiventer*) and in southern New Guinea (*N. p. evangelinae*); often found in gardens and parks with open water.

Habits: This very aggressive species always lives in pairs. The birds spend practically all their time in shrubbery, where they look for various grass seeds (genera *Sorghum, Panicum,* and *Iseilema*), insects, and spiders. They do not engage in any social grooming or contact sitting, habits that are very common in most species of exotic finches.

In the second half of the rainy season, Crimson Finches build their nests in palm trees or against buildings, using half decayed or soft leaves of grass or reeds. Both partners sit on the five to eight eggs. The young are fed insects—mostly termites and ants—that are caught on the wing.

Requirements in captivity: Since 1960, when Australia banned the export of exotic finches, all birds offered for sale have been bred in captivity. Cold and wet weather is highly pernicious for Crimson Finches, and they need temperatures of at least 65 to 68°F (18–20°C).

Unfortunately, Crimson Finches do not get along among themselves or with other species. They will attack and sometimes hound to death even parakeets and small pigeons. They consequently have to be kept in single pairs. Their aviary should contain some thick bushes or reeds because these birds do not like to be on the ground.

Food: Small-grained, large-grained, and spike millets, sprouted millet, lots of green seeds of wild grasses, chickweed, ant pupae, freshly hatched mealworms, fruit flies, and other small insects.

Breeding: The prerequisites for successful breeding are even temperatures of at least 68°F (20°C) and an especially nutritious rearing diet.

Crimson Finches build their nests out of grass leaves, bast, coconut fibers, and white feathers in recesses in a wall, on shelves, and occasionally in nesting boxes. After

When seeking food in the wild, Star Finches climb up on plant stalks or pick seeds out of seed heads.

11 to 14 days the young birds, covered with gray down, hatch, and the keeper now has to offer an especially varied diet.

The juvenile molt and a change in the bill's color set in at three months and last longer than in other exotic finches. During this time the birds are especially delicate and quite fussy about what they will eat.

Star Finch
Neochmia ruficauda

Description: 4¼ inches (11 cm).

Male: Forehead, lores, sides of head, and upper throat, scarlet with white dots on the throat and auricular regions; upper side, grayish green to olive green; wings, gray-brown; belly, greenish gray to olive green with round white dots; upper tail coverts and central tail feathers, crimson.

Female: Colors more muted than in the male; on the head only the forehead, front of cheeks, and chin are red.

Distribution and habitat: Large swampy areas with wild rice and wet grassland with some bushes and trees in northern Australia.

Habits: Except during breeding season, Star Finches live in groups. They prefer bushes to the ground. They pick seeds—mostly green grass seed—out of seed heads by climbing up a stalk and holding on tightly with their feet. Depending on the time of year they make flights from their perches to catch insects.

Breeding time comes during the rainy season. The nests are built in thick bushes. Grass stalks are used as building material and feathers as padding. The female lays three to six eggs. Both partners sit on the eggs and feed the young. The rearing diet consists primarily of insects.

Requirements in captivity: In the summer, Star Finches can be kept in an outdoor aviary, but since they do not sleep in nests, they need a room that protects them from the cold and wet even in the warm season. In the winter they can be briefly exposed to temperatures as low as 54 to 59°F (12–15°C). The aviary or cage should contain some thick bushes and tall grass or reeds for climbing.

Star Finches are quite good-natured and defend only their immediate nesting territory while breeding. If there is enough dense vegetation, several pairs can be kept together.

Food: Small- and large-grained and spike millets; green and sprouted seeds; small, freshly hatched mealworms; ant pupae.

Breeding: If there is sufficient dense shrubbery in the aviary, Star Finches will soon start to build nests, for which they need grass stalks and feathers. After 12 days of incubation the young birds with their gray down hatch. The parents now must be given plenty of animal proteins; otherwise, they refuse to feed the young.

After three weeks the young leave the nest. At first they still need an inside room to protect them, especially at night, against wetness and low temperatures. After another two weeks they are fully independent.

Zebra Finch
Poephila guttata

Description: 4 inches (10 cm).

Male: Crown and neck, light gray; back, mouse gray; lores and cheeks, which are set off by two vertical black lines, white; sides of head, rust red; throat and crop, silver gray with black crossbarring; front of breast, black; sides of body, reddish with round white dots; lower body, white.

Female: Like the male but sides of head are gray; throat, crop, and upper breast, gray; sides of body, mouse gray without spots.

Distribution and habitat: Open grassland dotted with bushes and trees and near water; dry savannas, open areas, pastures, and cultivated land all over Australia, except for northeastern Queensland and the southeastern and southwestern coast.

Habits: Zebra Finches live in groups year-round and feed mainly on grass seeds they pick off the ground.

The Zebra Finch is very popular among finch owners.

In the second half of the rainy season or whenever there has been sufficient rainfall they build their nests, preferably in thick, thorny bushes, in the substructure of aeries, near wasps' nests, or in tree holes. Dry grass stalks, soft grass, plant silks, and feathers serve as padding on which the four to six eggs are deposited. Both parents feed the young, giving them mostly green grass seeds and, less often, insects.

Outside the breeding season Zebra Finches spend the night in sleeping nests.

Requirements in captivity: The Zebra Finch is one of the most commonly held cage birds among exotic finches because it is one of the easiest birds to house and feed and therefore ideal for the beginning bird fancier. All birds for sale have been bred in captivity since Australia banned the export of birds in 1960. In the course of time different color variations have been obtained through selective breeding, the best known of these being the white and the silver-colored varieties.

Zebra Finches can be kept in pairs either in a large cage or in an aviary. If housed in the latter fashion, males sometimes seriously pester smaller, less vigorous species so that there should be enough bushes in the aviary to offer plenty of opportunities for getting out of the way and hiding.

Food: Small-grained millets, sprouted millet, greens, small mealworms, and insects.

Breeding: Zebra Finches will breed in large flight cages that are at least 3 feet (1 m) long. They like to build their nests in enclosed or semi-open nesting boxes, Harz boxes, or bast or rattan nests that can be bought at pet stores. It is rare at this point to see these birds nest in a natural setting. They need soft, dry grass and coconut fibers as building materials and feathers for padding.

The baby birds hatch after 12 to 14 days. They are covered with white down and, if given the right diet consisting of egg food and green seeds, grow up without problems. It may happen, however, that toward the end of the feeding period the parent birds get so absorbed in a new mating that they neglect or totally give up their feeding duties toward their nearly independent earlier brood. In such a case, you should temporarily remove all nests until the young can make it on their own. At that point they should be separated from their parents because quarrels will otherwise arise.

Young Zebra Finches mature early and sometimes attempt to mate as early as 11 or 12 weeks. It is better, however, not to let them breed until they are at least nine months old because earlier mating weakens the birds and produces offspring that are not very vigorous.

Bicheno Finch
Poephila bichenovii

Description: 4 inches (10 cm).

Male and female: Forehead and a band running from above the eyes down the sides of the head and across the throat, black; back and neck, pale brown with dark cross-barring; wings with checkerboard pattern; rump, black (white in the Ringed Finch [*P. b. annulosa annulosa*]); tail, brownish black; sides of head, throat, and belly, white; black band running across breast; under tail coverts, black.

Distribution and habitat: Steppes and savannas, grazing and cultivated land in northern Australia (*P. b. annulosa*), eastern and interior Australia (*P. b. bichenovii*); also in heavily settled areas, often seen in gardens and parks.

Habits: Bicheno Finches are agile climbers, but they also move about on the ground, where they look for grass and other plant seeds. These gregarious birds live in groups year-round and even sleep together in nests. They form large flocks only at times of drought.

In northern Australia, Bicheno Finches breed in the second half of the rainy period (when there is plenty of water and food) near farms and cultivated land. The raising of the young extends far into the dry period. The nests are built in the forked branches of bushes or small trees (at heights from 5 to 10 feet [1.5–3 m]) and made of stiff dry grass stalks and plant stems. In contrast to the northern Australian subspecies, birds of the eastern Australian subspecies (*P. b. bichenovii*) pad their nests with lots of feathers. A clutch consists of four to five eggs. Insects have to be available for feeding the young birds.

The Bicheno Finch is sometimes referred to as an Owl Finch because of its face coloration.

Requirements in captivity: Bicheno Finches are very sensitive to the cold and need even temperatures of 68 to 72°F (20–22°C). If they are kept in an outdoor aviary they have to have an inside room to retreat to during bad weather. The aviary has to be densely planted not only to offer enough nesting sites but also to do justice to the natural way of life of these birds. Bicheno Finches defend their immediate nesting area against other birds only during breeding time.

Food: Various millets, especially small-grained, spike, and sprouted millet; green seeds and small or freshly hatched mealworms.

Breeding: As a rule, Bicheno Finches raise their young successfully and build their nests in thick bushes. Grass and plant stems serve as building materials. These birds only rarely accept nesting boxes or Harz boxes.

A Masked Grassfinch in the wild.

The young hatch after 12 days. At this point, the parents have to be given plenty of fresh ant pupae, mealworms, aphids, and other small insects. They will not feed egg food or dried ant pupae to their young. Some pairs continue raising one brood after another. In order not to wear out the female or get weak, undernourished young birds, Bicheno Finches should be allowed to raise no more than three sets of young a year. The young of this species reach sexual maturity early but, for the reasons just mentioned, they should not be allowed to mate before they are nine months old.

Masked Grassfinch
Poephila personata

Description: 5½ inches (14 cm).

Male: Narrow black band across the forehead; lores, cheeks, chin, throat, black; upper rump, black with a black band extending down the sides; lower rump, white; upper side, reddish brown; sides of head,

depending on subspecies, purplish brown (*P. p. personata*) or white (*P. p. leucotis*); center of belly, white; rest of underside, a delicate purplish brown with a suggestion of fine crossbarring.

Female: Like male; black mask and band on side often smaller.

Distribution and habitat: Dry steppes, open savannas with occasional eucalyptus trees and thick undergrowth, brush steppes in northern Australia from Derby to the Cape York Peninsula; the subspecies *P. p. leucotis* occurs in northwestern Queensland and in the north of the Cape York Peninsula.

Habits: The Masked Grassfinches are among the most gregarious of Australia's exotic finches. They live in flocks all year-round, but the pairs stay close together within the flock. The birds spend most of the time on the ground, where they pick up green and ripe seeds and fly to the trees only for rest.

At the end of the rainy season, pairs build their nests in trees, bushes, and on the ground hidden below tufts of grass. Both parents collect nesting material and take turns building. Since they incorporate bits of charcoal in the nest, the eggs gradually turn black. The parents raise the five young primarily on termites caught in flight.

Requirements in captivity: As natives of host regions, Masked Grassfinches always need temperatures above 68 to 72°F (20–22°C). In a cooler environment they catch cold easily. They are not well suited for life in a cage because without sufficient room for flying they tend to get lazy. In an aviary, several pairs should always be housed together because these birds are very fussy in choosing partners.

Food: Various kinds of millet, especially large-grained millet, also canary, sprouted millet, green seeds, chickweed, ant pupae, small mealworms.

Breeding: Masked Greenfinches are easily frightened at all stages of the breeding cycle, and any disturbance should therefore be avoided. Usually, the pairs build their nests in thick bushes, dense pine branches, or semiopen nesting boxes. Coconut fibers and various grasses are good building materials, as well as hairs and feathers for padding. Once the young hatch, the parents have to be supplied with plenty of greens and animal proteins.

Even though the young birds seem ready earlier, they must not be separated from their parents before their juvenile molt or they stop eating.

Long-tailed Grassfinch
Poephilia acuticauda

Description: 6¾ inches (17 cm).

Male and female: Lores, black; head and nape, a delicate bluish gray; broad black band across rump and extending down the sides of the body; rump and upper tail coverts, white; tail, black and tapered with two very long central feathers; throat and crop area, black; upper side, a delicate pinkish brown; belly, a paler shade of the same hue.

Distribution and habitat: Dry steppes and eucalyptus savannas in northern Australia from Derby and the Fitzroy River to the Gulf of Carpentaria in northwestern Queensland.

Habits: Long-tailed Grassfinches live in groups year-round but individual pairs stay close together within the group. They get their food— green and ripe seeds of grasses such as *Eriachne obtusa* and various *Eragrotsis* species—almost exclusively from the ground.

During breeding time, which falls into the rainy season, Long-tailed Grassfinches live almost entirely on swarming termites and ants. They build their nests in the branches of tall trees. The basic building material is grass stalks; plant silks and white feathers provide a soft layer under the five to six eggs. The parents feed their young almost exclusively with insects.

Two Long-tailed Grassfinches resting on a branch.

Requirements in captivity: If kept properly, Long-tailed Grassfinches present no special problems. They can manage in temperatures as low as 60°F (15°C), but like other exotic finches, they react adversely to humid cold. A pair of these birds can be kept in a large flight cage that is at least 3 feet (1 m) long, and they will even breed there. It is not advisable to keep more than one pair of this species in an aviary. Though they live communally in the wild, life in captivity does not offer enough chance for the birds to get away from one another, and fierce conflicts can arise between individual birds. But Long-tailed Grassfinches get along peacefully with other exotic finches except for the closely related Parson and Masked Finches.

Food: Various kinds of millet, canary, sprouted millet, green grass seed, chickweed, small mealworms.

Breeding: Long-tailed Grassfinches are characterized by especially close bonding between pairs, many of which stay together as long as they live. Individual birds are very picky about choosing mates and should be allowed to select a partner to their liking from a group. An arranged match may not produce offspring for years because of mutual antipathy, but if birds have their own choice, they breed without complications. In captivity, Long-tailed Grassfinches show no particular preference for artificial or natural nesting sites. Consequently, they should have dense bushes as well as enclosed or semiopen nesting boxes at their disposal. Coconut fibers, long stalks of grass or hay, and strips of bast are used as building materials, and lots of white feathers as padding. The young hatch after 13 to 14 days and are ready to leave the nest when they are three weeks old. At this point they are especially susceptible to the cold and wet and should be brought into a warm room at night and during rainy spells.

The attachment of Long-tailed Grassfinches is very strong not only between mates but also between parents and their young. If young birds are separated from their parents when they have reached independence but before the juvenile molt, they often fail to adjust to their new surroundings and may starve to death in the presence of full food dishes. When they are three and a half months old, the family can safely be broken up.

Parson Finch
Poephila cincta

Description: 4¼ inches (11 cm). Male and female: Crown and sides of head and neck, light blue-gray; back and wings, pinkish brown; rump and upper tail coverts, white or black, depending on subspecies; tail, throat, and crop area, black; belly, light shade of pinkish brown; black band across sides of lower body.

Distribution and habitat: Open savannas with scattered eucalyptus trees near water in northeastern Australia from the Cape York Peninsula southward through Queensland to the northernmost parts of New South Wales.

Habits: The species feeds primarily on grass seeds and other seeds. The birds live in flocks year-round, and pairs nest closely together. Their breeding is not tied to any particular season, and nests with eggs are therefore found at any time of year after sufficient rainfalls.

Parson Finches build their nests in tall eucalyptus trees, abandoned kingfisher caves, termite nests, and, with particular preference, in aeries. They use dry grass, plant silks, and white feathers as a lining. A clutch consists of five to nine eggs and is thus one of the largest among Australian finches. The parent birds feed the young primarily termites, which they catch on the wing.

Requirements in captivity: Like Long-tailed Grassfinches, Parson Finches do not do well if exposed to temperatures below 60°F (15°C) or to cool, damp conditions; otherwise, they are easy to keep and breed. Although they live in gregarious communities in the wild, their aggressiveness toward others of their kind is even more pronounced than in their Long-tailed cousins. It is practically impossible to keep several pairs or one pair together with other species of exotic finches in one aviary because there is not enough room for the birds to get out of each other's way. Parson Finches can be housed communally only with larger birds such as serins, siskins, or Shama Thrushes; or pairs can be kept singly in large flight cages.

A Parson Finch observing the ground from a tree branch.

Food: Large-grained millet, canary, green seeds, egg food, mealworms.

Breeding: As in all *Poephila* species, the bonding between Parson Finches is very close. Two mates like to spend practically all their time together. But it is very difficult to get an arbitrarily matched pair to breed. The best thing is to let the birds pick their own partners.

Unlike Long-tailed Grassfinches, Parson Finches like to move into enclosed nesting boxes, since in the wild they quite often nest in caves. They need coconut fibers, bast, blades of grass, moss, and other building materials. The young hatch after 12 days and need a lot of green and sprouted seeds as rearing food. They are quite immature even when they leave the nest and—like their Long-tailed cousins—they cannot be separated from their parents before the juvenile molt, which sets in at about six to eight weeks.

115

Pintailed Parrot Finches do best in captivity when housed in large aviaries.

Parson Finches reach sexual maturity rather early, but to prevent debilitation they should not be allowed to breed until they are 9 to 12 months old.

Pintailed Parrot Finch
Erythrura prasina

Description: 6 inches (15 cm).

Male: Forehead, sides of head, and throat, blue; lores, blackish; nape and back, green; wing feathers, blackish brown; rump and central tail feathers, which form the point of the tail, red; other tail feathers, blackish brown; breast, vivid red; belly, yellowish cinnamon color.

Female: The parts of the head that are blue and the parts of the body that are green in the male are both a subdued green in the female; belly, brownish ocher to gray.

Distribution and habitat: Edge of forests, bamboo thickets, and rice fields at moderate altitudes from Laos and northern Thailand southward to Malaysia, Java, Sumatra, and Borneo.

Habits: Pintailed Parrot Finches live on grass seeds and in some seasons almost exclusively on ripening rice. When it is not time to breed, the birds live in small flocks.

The nests, which consist of small roots, dry leaves, and plant fibers are built in bushes, bamboo grass, or on trees and lined with softer materials. The female lays four to six eggs, and the young are raised on green seeds.

Requirements in captivity: Pintailed Parrot Finches, too, tend to obesity if kept in cages and usually die within a few months. They are happiest in a large and well-planted aviary, living together with other kinds of exotic finches or possibly with several members of their own species.

Under these conditions, the birds give each other cause to move about. But aviaries with glass walls should be avoided because these birds scare easily and can get hurt when flying against the glass. Pintailed Parrot Finches are very sensitive to the cold. They do not sleep in nests and need temperatures from 61 to 68°F (16–20°C) and, during the breeding season, as high as 77°F (25°C).

Food: Canary, hulled oats, peeled oats, various kinds of millet, sprouted canary and oats, lots of green grass seeds (annual bluegrass, panic grass), sprouted wheat, ant pupae, scalded mealworms.

Breeding: One complicating factor in trying to breed Pintailed Parrot Finches is that both males and females molt twice annually. Only if the molting cycle of the two birds coincides can they both get ready to mate at the same time. Most pairs build nests in thick bushes, broom branches, or tufts of tall grass, and they require coconut fibers, bast, narrow leaves, and soft blades of grass as building materials. A clutch consists of only two to five eggs, and usually no more than two to three young hatch. The parent birds feed them quite diligently if they are given sufficient green seeds and greens. The female stops keeping the nestlings under her wing as early as after eight to ten days, and at this point a heater (not a heat lamp that emits not only warmth but also light) should be placed near the nest to keep the nestlings from getting too cold during the next few days.

Blue-faced Parrot Finch

Erythrura trichroa

Description: 4¾ inches (12 cm).

Male: Grass green with upper side darker, underside lighter, often tending toward yellowish; forehead and sides of head, blue; rump and upper tail coverts, red; central tail feathers, red and somewhat longer than the others, which are blackish brown.

Female: Like the male but often somewhat muted; less blue on the head.

Distribution and habitat: Mountain woods, gardens, tree plantations, open grassland in New Guinea, on the Molucca Islands, Celebes, Micronesia, the New Hebrides, the Cape York Peninsula in Australia, and parts of the Bismarck Archipelago.

Habits: Outside of the breeding season, Blue-faced Parrot Finches often live in large flocks, but during

The Blue-faced Parrot Finch often lives in large flocks.

the mating season they always show up in pairs. They like to forage for food among low bushes and grass, where they pick seeds out of bamboo and grass seed heads. They do this by landing on flexible grass stalks, pushing them down to the ground, and holding onto them with their feet while they pick out the seeds.

This species builds oval-shaped nests in bushes or trees with thick foliage, often mango trees. Blades of grass, ferns, dry leaves, moss, and mycelium are used for nesting materials and together with grass and small roots they are piled up to form a pad on which the female lays her three to six eggs. The baby birds are raised on insects.

Requirements in captivity: These birds are best kept in a very large aviary that contains both dense plantings for climbing around and nesting in and generous open areas for flying. Since they come from tropical forests, these birds need temperatures between 61 and 68°F (16–20°C) and somewhat higher when there are young birds that have left the nest.

Blue-faced Parrot Finches are a good bet for a mixed community of exotic finches because they are generally good-natured even during mating time. There are, however, a few obnoxious individuals that seek out breeding pairs of their own or another species in their nests and pester them.

Food: Primarily green and soaked seeds (this species eats dry seeds only reluctantly), canary, millet, oats, wheat, lots of greens, fruit, ant pupae, mealworms.

Breeding: These birds nest in semiopen as well as enclosed boxes and occasionally in bushes. They prefer building their nests out of coconut fibers, blades of grass, or moss, and pad them with soft plant materials. Incubation takes 12 to 14 days. The parent birds regularly remove the droppings of the nestlings so that the nest stays clean until the young leave it after three weeks. When this happens, the room temperature has to be raised somewhat for a few days.

Like their Red-throated relatives, Blue-faced Parrot Finches attempt to mate very early but should not get a chance to build a nest until they are eight months old.

Red-headed Parrot Finch
Erythrura psittacea

Description: 4¾ inches (12 cm).

Male: Head, bright red; upper tail coverts and central tail feathers, red; back and belly, grass green.

Female: Like the male but usually more muted; the red face mask is smaller and lighter in color.

Distribution and habitat: Grassland, shrubbery, and abandoned plantations on New Caledonia.

Habits: When not breeding, Red-headed Parrot Finches live together in groups. They pick up their food not only off the ground but also by climbing up stalks of grass and picking the grass seeds out of the seed heads.

This species breeds at any time of year. The birds build their nests in trees and bushes as well as on beams and in recesses of buildings. Stalks of grass provide the building material. Both partners sit on the eggs, and they feed the young on a diet made up exclusively of animal proteins until shortly before they leave the nest.

Requirements in captivity: Life in a cage is not for Red-headed Parrot Finches because it either makes them stay wild and shy or causes them to become lazy and obese. But they are excellent members of an aviary community, where they become quite friendly and get along well with all kinds of other birds. Since they are fast and agile flyers, the aviary has to offer large open areas in addition to thickly planted corners. These birds react badly to the cold and have to be kept at a minimum temperature of 65°F (18°C). During the initial adjustment period and at breeding time, they require 68°F (20°C).

Food: Scalded mealworms, enchytraeids, ant pupae, egg food, some fruit (apples, oranges, figs), lots of greens and green seeds, chickweed, knotweed, small-grained millet, canary, peeled oats (both dry and soaked). This species is much more vegetarian than other Parrot Finches.

Breeding: If fed a proper diet, these Parrot Finches are unproblematic to breed, but it is not always easy to pick out a pair. One good way to tell the sex is to listen to the

Red-headed Parrot Finches build their nests in trees and shrubs.

mating call, which consists of a long-drawn-out trill in the case of a male. The female emits a much shorter call. The pair will start building their nest promptly, preferably in semiopen or enclosed nesting boxes, though they sometimes locate their nests in thick bushes, too. They accept coconut fibers, grass stalks, bast, and dry leaves but favor long fibers (8 to 12 inches [20-30 cm]). The female lays 4 to 6 eggs, which hatch after 13 days. The young are almost naked and need plenty of ant pupae, egg food, and mealworms to survive. The parent birds protect them only for a few days, and the temperature in the aviary therefore has to be at least 68°F (20°C) so that the nestlings will not catch cold at night.

The young leave the nest after three weeks, and after another two weeks they are independent. They are ready to mate as early as three

The Gouldian Finch is one of the most spectacularly colored finches.

consists mostly of partially and fully ripe sorghum seeds. They climb up the stalks and pick the maturing seeds out of the seed heads. But they also consume more termites, beetles, and spiders than other Australian finches and live on an exclusive diet of these during the breeding season.

Gouldian Finches live in small, loose colonies during breeding time, which comes during the second half of the rainy season for them. Usually they adopt abandoned brooding caves left by parakeets and simply deposit their eggs on the detritus there, or they use holes in trees. If they build nests, which they construct from various grasses, they do not line them.

Requirements in captivity: Gouldian Finches inhabit the hottest parts of Australia, and in order for them to perk up and become active, they need to be kept at 77°F (25°C) or warmer in captivity. They also require a high air humidity of 55 to 70 percent. They do not thrive if they are kept exclusively in cages, because they often suffer from metabolic problems if they do not get enough exercise. Gouldian Finches get along well with each other and with other exotic finches. Since they spur each other's mating instinct and since the free choice of a partner has a beneficial effect on their breeding, it is desirable to keep several pairs together.

Food: Canary, small- and large-grained millet, partially ripe and/or sprouted spike millet, green grass

to four months after hatching, but they should be segregated by sex in aviaries without nesting sites to prevent premature broods.

Gouldian Finch
Chloebia gouldiae

Description: 6 inches (15 cm).

Male: Crown and sides of head, scarlet red bordered by a black line; a wide light blue band across back of head; nape and sides of neck, light green; back and wings, a purple-blue; belly, yellow; legs and under tail coverts, white.

Female: Colors more muted, and the blue band across the back of the head is narrower or lacking. The Gouldian Finch also occurs with a black or a yellow head.

Distribution and habitat: Dry eucalyptus savannas in northern Australia with the exception of the Cape York Peninsula.

Habits: Gouldian Finches live in groups all year-round. Their food seeds (annual bluegrass, English ryegrass), prostrate knotweed, chickweed, mealworms, and perhaps egg food.

Breeding: Most Gouldian Finches accept enclosed or semiopen nesting boxes (minimum size: 6 × 6 × 6 inches [15 × 15 × 15 cm]) mounted as high as possible. Since many captive birds no longer build nests, the keeper has to see to it that the boxes are well supplied with nesting materials so that the eggs will not get crushed. The birds like sisal, coconut fibers, bast, soft hay, and moss best for building. The young hatch after 14 to 15 days, and they should be fed with a great variety of partially ripe seeds and animal foods. The female keeps the nestlings warm only until the tenth day, and the temperature must not be allowed to drop below 68°F (20°C) at this point. The young birds should not be separated from their parents until they enter the juvenile molt at six to eight weeks of age. If moved earlier, they often cannot find their way around in a new environment.

Cherry Finch

Aidemosyne modesta

Description: 4¼ inches (11 cm).

Male: Lores, black; forehead and front of crown, dark crimson; top of head, dark brown; upper side, gray-brown with white crossbarring on the rump; wing coverts with white tips; chin and throat, reddish black; side of head, white with pale brown crossbarring; belly, white with pale brown zebra stripes.

An alert Cherry Finch perching on a shrub branch.

Female: Crimson area of forehead smaller; chin and upper throat, white; zebra stripes on belly less pronounced.

Distribution and habitat: Grassland, scrubland, swamps, and reed stands in interior eastern Australia from Queensland to New South Wales.

Habits: Cherry Finches are found only near water, and because of the progressive drying up of their habitat, their range keeps shrinking. During extensive droughts, the birds move far into other regions in their search for water. They live in pairs only during the breeding season; at other times they form huge flocks. They find their food—seeds of grass and other plants—on the ground or pick it directly out of the seed heads.

In the rainy season—or at other times if there is enough water and food—the pairs build nests in tufts of grass, low bushes, blackberry tangles, or among stalks of grass or woody twigs that stand straight up. The four to seven eggs are laid on a base of grass stalks, and the young are reared on insects.

Requirements in captivity: Cherry Finches have a great need for warmth. Freshly imported birds must be kept at 72°F (22°C) at the beginning, and after they are acclimated at 65°F (18°C). Since they tend to become sluggish if kept in a cage, it is best to house them in a fair-sized aviary with reeds and grass. They defend their nests against other birds—both of their own and of other species—only during mating season.

Food: Small- and large-grained millets, sprouted millet, greens.

Breeding: If you hope to raise young Cherry Finches, you should be aware of several facts: Any disturbance of these extremely sensitive birds during the incubation period will cause them to abandon the eggs. "Personal antipathies" often prevent mating altogether. It is therefore important to keep a number of birds together so that they can choose their own partners. Quite often, parent birds will neglect their still dependent young when the urge to mate again wakens. In contrast to many other exotic finches, which let different broods overlap, Cherry Finches usually stop feeding their offspring when building a new nest. The only way to prevent this is to make sure there is no other nesting site around or to move the family to another aviary. If all these factors

are taken into account, Cherry Finches make good parents. They like to build their nests out of coconut fibers and soft blades of grass and locate them in thick bushes or in among reeds and tall grass. The female usually lays four eggs. For feeding the young, they need fresh ant pupae, small mealworms, and insects, as well as green and sprouted seeds.

African Silverbill

Euodice malabarica cantans (a subspecies of the Indian Silverbill [*E. malabarica*])

Description: 4¼ inches (11 cm).

Male and female: Crown and back, light yellowish brown with darker stripes on the head and darker crossbarring on the back; rump and upper tail coverts, black; sides of head and throat, light yellowish brown; breast and sides a duller shade of the same color; wings and tail, blackish brown; eyelids with bluish gray rim (not present in the Indian Silverbill).

Distribution and habitat: Dry savannas and semidesert, often near cultivated land in the northern parts of tropical Africa south of the Sahara; in eastern Africa from Somalia to central Tanzania; southwestern Arabia.

Habits: African Silverbills live in dry regions and often form large flocks outside of mating season. They feed on grass and other seeds, picking them off the ground and out of the seed heads that they pull down to get at the kernels.

The mating season occurs in the second half of the rainy period but birds also breed in the dry season. They build their nests in thornbushes or trees, under roofs or on verandas. Grass stalks and sprays are used for building, and the inside of the nest is lined with fine grass, feathers, hairs, and plant silks. The four to five young are raised mostly on green seeds.

Requirements in captivity: African and Indian Silverbills are easy to keep and feed and can therefore be recommended for beginners. They show how interesting and varied their social life can be only if they are allowed to live in pairs or groups in an aviary. Since they are eager and skillful climbers, they should have a thicket of branches as well as large flying areas at their disposal. Both species get along well among themselves and with other birds, though there may be some flights to defend the nest during breeding time.

Food: Large- and small-grained millets, spike millet, lots of greens, maturing seeds, egg food.

Breeding: The African Silverbill is one of the most reliable breeders among African finches. If the partners pick each other out of a group they stay together for years and will raise several broods annually.

These birds will build nests in natural sites or move into enclosed or semiopen nesting boxes or baskets. They need coconut fibers, bast, and grass or hay stalks, and pad the nest

Two African Silverbills relaxing on a twig.

with feathers. The young are raised on egg food and green seeds. The young birds leave the nest at 21 days and quite quickly—compared to other species—become remarkably accomplished fliers. At any disturbance and at night, the parents call the young birds back to the nest.

The Indian Silverbill *(E. malabarica)*, which has the same requirements for care and feeding as the African subspecies, has a stronger, more vivid brown coloring on the head. In the wild, this bird lives near fields, in gardens and towns, on steppes, and in grass thickets in India and on Sri Lanka (Ceylon).

Bronze Mannikin
Lonchura cucullata

Description: 3½ inches (9 cm).

Male and female: Head, black with a metallic green sheen; back and wings, earth brown; recently molted primaries have narrow light outlines that can suggest a checkerboard pattern; shoulders have a black spot; tail, black; belly, white with brown sides where wide bands on feathers form crossbarring; under tail coverts white with blackish brown crossbarring.

Distribution and habitat: Thornbush steppes, swamps, dry savannas, clearings, and forests along rivers in Africa south of the Sahara. Several races.

Habits: When not breeding, the Bronze Mannikins live in close-knit flocks on the outskirts of towns. They eat small grass seeds, picking them off the ground or off plants. They also consume termites that they catch on the wing. At night the individual families sleep in old brood nests.

Bronze Mannikins usually breed in the warm season; those that live near the equator, at any time of year. Nests are generally built in small

The Bronze Mannikin is an African species that lives south of the Sahara Desert.

trees (mango and orange trees), often right next to wasps' nests, but also under the roofs of buildings. Fine grass, inflorescences, and seed heads are used for padding. Bronze Mannikins may also move into abandoned weavers' nests. They lay four to six eggs and feed their young green seeds.

Requirements in captivity: Because these birds have such modest demands, they are a good bet for beginners. They sometimes even breed in a cage, but prolonged cage life makes them sluggish and dull. Anyone who wants to get to know the full range of behavior of these sociable little birds and wants to create ideal conditions for them should keep a pair or a group of them in an aviary. However, the males occasionally become aggressive at mating time and should be carefully watched.

Food: Mixed millets, spike millet, sprouted millet, lots of greens, possibly egg food, mealworms, ant pupae.

Breeding: Bronze Mannikins can produce offspring regularly and unproblematically, but they should be allowed to choose their mates from a group. They normally use semiopen nesting boxes or Harz boxes but sometimes build in bushes. They should be given coconut fibers, grass stalks and leaves, and grass and cotton for padding. After 12 to 14 days the baby birds hatch and now need lots of greens and animal proteins. The rearing diet should be especially varied or the parent birds may reject their young. The fledglings leave the nest at three weeks.

If the young birds are left together with their parents, an extended family develops in the course of successive broods. Even during the mating season, the members will never display enough aggression toward each other to warrant removal of birds.

The closest relatives of this species are the Magpie Mannikin (L. fringilloides), 4¾ inches (12 cm), and the Blue-billed Manninkin (L. bicolor), 3½ inches (9 cm), both of which need the same care and feeding as the Bronze Mannikin. Both these species also have a great need for company since they live in large flocks in the wild.

The Magpie Mannikin has a black head, dark brown back, white breast and belly, and black sides with a brown patch. These birds come from forests in Africa south of the Sahara.

The head and neck of the Blue-billed Mannikin are glossy greenish black, the rest of the upper side, brown or black according to subspecies. Primaries and secondaries are black, but the Blue-billed Mannikin has a dense white sprinkling that gives a crosshatched effect. The belly is white with black feathers rimmed in white on the sides. This species lives in clearings and on the edge of forests across wide areas of tropical Africa from Portuguese Guinea to Zambia and southern Ethiopia.

White-backed Munia
Lonchura striata

Description: 4¼ to 4¾ inches (11–12 cm).

Male and female: Forehead, crown, and throat, black; back, brown; tail, brownish black and wedge-shaped with sharply pointed central tail feathers; crop area and upper breast, black or dark brown; lower belly, white, in some races with grayish brown spots. Ten subspecies.

Distribution and habitat: Wooded grasslands, clearings near rice fields, also village gardens in Ceylon, India, Burma, Malaysia, Sumatra, southern China as far north as the Yangtse River, Taiwan.

Habits: White-backed Munias live in groups even during the mating season and often form huge flocks at other times of year. They eat grass and other seeds, rice, and berries directly off the plant.

White-backed Munias breed during the rainy season and build their nests in bushes and trees. They pile up fine grass rather carelessly and lay their four to eight eggs without padding the nest. The young are fed primarily with ripening seeds, and the nest is later used by the whole family as a sleeping nest.

Requirements in captivity: These birds have been kept and bred in Europe since the seventeenth century. Except during the mating season, they coexist peacefully in groups, but when brooding, mutual "visiting" can become such a nuisance that individual pairs have to be removed and housed separately.

Food: Mixed millet seeds, greens, sprouted seeds, egg food.

Breeding: White-backed Munias can be bred in an aviary at any time of year, even in winter, but because fresh greens are necessary and the birds should not be debilitated, it is best to restrict the breeding to the summer months. The birds build their nests in thick bushes or bunches of pine or broom branches but also use semiopen nesting boxes that have to be extra large since the parent birds often amass great amounts of nesting material. Often the bottom of the nest is on a level with the entrance, and a departing parent bird can easily knock out eggs or a nestling by mistake. To prevent this, you should make the hollow of the nest a little deeper with your hand.

The parents feed their young quite conscientiously with egg food and large amounts of sprouted and green seeds. In captivity the young birds molt at 7 to 11 weeks. A report that in the wild the juvenile molt does not set in until the birds are five months old is questionable if only because it includes no reliable method for establishing the age of a young bird.

Bengalese Finch

Lonchura striata (domesticated form)
Description: 4¼ to 4¾ inches (11–12 cm).

This is the domesticated form of the White-backed Munia. We assume that it evolved several hundred years ago from the Chinese subspecies *L. striata swinhoei* and was then imported to Japan, where selective breeding produced many variations in coloration and in plumage pattern.

There are three basic types of coloration: brown mottled, yellow mottled, and white. ("Mottled" here means that there are more or less blotches of white.) Even within one type of coloration, the shade, intensity, and distribution of colors can vary widely. White Bengalese Finches either have dark eyes (there is pigment in the iris) or are true albinos with red eyes. White birds, especially albinos, easily develop eye problems, but this can be prevented by giving them foods high in carotene, such as greens. If you are interested in breeding white Bengalese Finches, you should make sure to mate only healthy birds.

In the 1930s a new strain of crested Bengalese Finch was introduced, and since then it has been produced in all color variations.

Requirements in captivity: In contrast to all other exotic finches, Bengalese Finches are better bred in cages than in aviaries. This is because they are especially sociable during the breeding period and like to crowd together in one nest without regard for the safety of the eggs. Or all the females will deposit their eggs in the same nest and get into each other's way incubating. That is why mating pairs should always be quartered separately.

At other times this species, too, should, because of its marked sociability, be kept in groups. But the birds should be segregated by sex to prevent unplanned breeding. Bengalese Finches that spend all their time in a cage tend to get lethargic and dull.

Food: Small- and large-grained millet, canary, greens, egg food.

Breeding: Bengalese Finches are probably the most reliable breeders among exotic finches. They start building nests within a few days of being placed in a brooding cage. They like enclosed or semiopen nesting boxes, in which they build loosely constructed nests of coconut fibers and grass. They return immediately to their eggs after a nest check. The young take 16 days to hatch and require a lot of chickweed, green seeds, and egg food.

The young birds should be separated from their parents once they become independent because otherwise, they want to continue sleeping in their old nest and interfere with the next brood.

Spice Finch

Lonchura punctulata

Description: 4¾ inches (12 cm).

Male and female: Head and throat (or cheek and throat, depending on race), reddish; sides of neck and upper side, reddish chocolate or duller brown; back and wing coverts, with whitish shaft lines; rump and tail, various markings and shades according to subspecies; belly, white with brown edges on feathers falling

A Bengalese Finch checking out a flowering plant.

scallop pattern on breast and sides. Twelve subspecies.

Distribution and habitat: Wild growth of grass and weeds, gardens on the outskirts of villages, near rice fields on Ceylon, in India, Indochina, southern China, on Formosa, Luzon, Palawan, Malaysia, Sumatra, Java, Bali, Celebes, and the Lesser Sunda Islands.

Habits: These sociable birds usually form small groups, sometimes together with members of other *Lonchura* species. They pick their food—mostly grass seeds—off the ground and, during harvest season, they eat the maturing rice kernels directly off the plants.

A number of pairs of Spice Finches often build nests apartment-style in bushes or on a bed of palm leaves. They use grass, straw, and bamboo leaves for building and raise their four to seven nestlings on green seeds.

Requirements in captivity: Spice Finches are ideal birds for beginning aviarists. They easily adjust to cage or aviary life and are relatively hardy, undemanding, and very peaceful. The only drawback in keeping them in cages is that they rarely raise offspring successfully there.

The cage or aviary should contain some leafy branches or dense bushes for nesting and some reeds or tall grass for climbing around on. Like all finches that come from reedy vegetation, Spice Finches have claws that grow too long—especially in a cage—and have to be trimmed periodically.

Food: Mixed millet, spike millet, lots of greens, egg food, mealworms, ant pupae.

Breeding: As with all other highly sociable species, harmony between the couple is a crucial factor in successful breeding. That is why you should let the birds choose their own partners out of a larger group.

Spice Finches like to build their voluminous nests on forked branches in dense vegetation. They need long and broad leaves of grass, flexible plant stems, roots, and, in some cases, coconut fibers. The hollow of the nest is padded with soft grass and moss. The parents raise their three to seven young primarily on sprouted seeds, greens, and immature seeds, as well as on egg food, mealworms, and ant pupae.

Chestnut Munia
Lonchura malacca

The species *Lonchura malacca* at present comprises several variant forms, some of which differ widely in

Spice Finches are ideal for novice bird owners because they are peaceful and easy to keep.

coloration and have in the past been considered different species or sub-species. The present classification can by no means be considered final because there are still few scientific studies on the relationship between the Black-headed Munia, the Tri-colored Munia, and the Javan White-headed Munia. Since, in the wild, these three variants are widely separated geographically, the question of how they interrelate has to be answered on the basis of observation in captivity. The three varieties mentioned are the ones usually sold at pet stores, and only these will be discussed here.

Description: 4¼ to 4¾ inches (11–12 cm).

Head and neck, black (in Javan White-headed Munia: head, white; neck black); back, wings, and rump, reddish; tail, brown; center of belly, black or brownish black; lower body, reddish (white in the Tri-colored Munia).

Distribution and habitat: Grassy regions, stands of reeds, and scrub brush in southern India and Ceylon (Tri-colored Munia); from eastern Nepal across Assam to western Burma (Black-headed Munia); and on Java and Bali (Javan White-headed Munia).

Habits: Outside of the mating season, Chestnut Munias stay together in social groups in cultivated areas, tall grass, reeds, or marshy brush. They eat grass seeds and rice kernels both off the ground and by climbing up the stems and picking them out of the bent-down seed heads.

Chestnut Munias are found in India.

Chestnut Munias breed mostly during the rainy season and build their nests in bushes, reeds, or rice fields. Leaves of grass and reeds as well as flowering grass are made into a nest for the four to six eggs. The young birds are raised on ripening seeds.

Requirements in captivity: In a cage all the different varieties of Munias tend to become inactive and rarely ever breed. That is why they should always be kept in groups in an aviary, particularly since they are well suited for living in mixed communities. At least one of the aviary's corners should have a dense growth of reeds or grass so that the birds will be able to find hidden nesting sites.

White-haired Munias are found in Malaysia.

Food: Large-grained millet, canary, sprouted and green seeds, chickweed.

Breeding: If Chestnut Munias are expected to produce offspring in captivity, the aviary has to offer quiet and protected nesting sites, and the birds have to be able to select their partners themselves. Arbitrarily matched pairs never mate.

The nests are usually built among dense reeds or tufts of grass or in thick bushes, and fresh as well as dry grasses, hairs, and sisal fibers are used as building materials.

After 12 to 15 days the young hatch and are fed sprouted and green seeds, which must be made available in great variety and abundance at this time. The adult pairs

only rarely accept animal proteins, but it is a good idea to at least try giving them hard-boiled eggs and mealworms.

The young birds leave their parents at six to seven weeks, later than other species.

White-haired Munia
Lonchura maja

Description: 4¼ inches (11 cm).

Male: head and neck, white; back and wings, dull chestnut; tail, black-brown; breast and sides of belly, chestnut brown; center of belly, black.

Female: the white on the head is less pure.

Distribution and habitat: Grassy areas, rice fields, and thick weeds on green mountain slopes on the Malay Peninsula and on the islands of Sumatra, Java, and Bali.

Habits: White-headed Munias live in pairs only during breeding season; the rest of the year they roam in large flocks. They live mostly on ripening rice and grass seeds, which they pick off the plants. Nests are built of roots, grass stalks, and other thin plant stems and located in the grass or bushes. The female lays four to six eggs, and both parents share in feeding the nestlings green seeds and insects.

Requirements in captivity: These undemanding and long-lived birds are a good addition to any mixed community of exotic finches. As in the case of Chestnut-breasted Finches, it is better to keep several pairs of them because, even more than in other species, they encourage each other's nest-building instinct. After some time in captivity, these birds tend to become lazy and should therefore be housed in an aviary if at all possible.

Food: Various millets, canary, some mixed birdseed, green and sprouted seeds.

Breeding: Birds that were caught in the wild only rarely breed in an aviary, but those born in captivity— as well as originally wild ones that have previously reproduced in captivity—make good and reliable parents. They should always be given the chance to pick their own partners. Nests are built in shrubbery or in a semiopen nesting box. Coarse grass and coconut fibers go into the building of the outer layers. The young hatch after 12 to 13 days and need large amounts of green seeds, egg food, mealworms, daphnia, aphids, and ant pupae for food.

At three weeks old, the young leave the nest but return to it at night for another month.

Gray-headed Munia
Lonchura caniceps

Description: Male and female: crown, gray; lores, blackish gray; throat and up the cheeks to auricular regions, gray with white-tipped feathers making a "pearled" black-and-white bib; neck, gray with blackish crossbarring; back, a dull cinnamon brown; crop, breast, and sides, cinnamon brown fading into white toward the back; wings, dark blackish brown; tail, black; rump and tail coverts, white.

Gray-headed Munias are difficult to breed in captivity.

Distribution and habitat: Dry thornbush savannas from southern Ethiopia to southeastern Kenya and in Tanzania from Iringa to south of Lake Victoria.

Habits: In the wild, Gray-headed Munias live on grass seeds. Not much else is known about them since their habits are reclusive.

Gray-headed Munias build large, rather untidy nests in the outer branches of trees. These nests are made up of grass stalks and are lined on the inside with feathers. The four to five young are fed seeds and insects.

Requirements in captivity: These birds soon become lethargic in a cage. They are rarely bred in captivity but make good members of a mixed community since they are peaceful and very sociable. They are so eager for contact that breeding pairs often visit each other's nests and spend the night together in one nest, sometimes at the cost of ruining the brood. That is why these birds should be kept in pairs when breeding and in groups at other times. Since Gray-headed Munias like to build nests in natural sites, they need some patches of thick vegetation in the aviary.

Food: Mixed millet, spike millet, sprouted millet, greens of all sorts but especially chickweed; also animal proteins such as mealworms, ant pupae, and waxmoth larvae.

Breeding: Like other species, Gray-headed Munias resist arbitrary pairing and breed only rarely under those conditions. That is why pairs should be allowed to form voluntarily in a group. These birds nest in enclosed and semiopen nesting boxes or in thick bushes. They need coconut fibers, leaves and stalks of grass, small pieces of shredded linen, moss, and feathers for building. Three to six birds hatch after 16 days and are raised without problems by the parents as long as enough ant pupae, waxmoth larvae, and mealworms are available. The young are 24 to 28 days old before they leave the nest.

Yellow-rumped Finch

Lonchura flaviprymna

Description: 4¼ inches (11 cm).

Male and female: Crown, back of head, and nape, whitish gray; back and wing coverts, chestnut brown; primaries and secondaries, grayish brown; belly, yellowish; breast, brownish ocher; rump and central tail feathers, yellow ocher; tail feathers, blackish brown.

Distribution and habitat: Wet lowlands; marshy areas; rice, sugarcane, and grain fields in northern and northwestern Australia; in coastal areas only during droughts, otherwise, in the interior.

Habits: Yellow-rumped Finches, sometimes together with the closely related Chestnut-breasted Finches, often form huge flocks; but since they do not live in heavily settled eastern Australia like their cousins, they are much shyer of people. They live mostly on ripening seed that they pick off the plants.

This species breeds during the second half of the rainy season, often in colonies. The nests are built in reeds or tall grass. Long blades of grass and seed heads are piled up in a nest for the four to five eggs. The nestlings are fed insects.

Yellow-rumped Finches readily crossbreed with their Chestnut-breasted cousins, and these two species should therefore preferably not be kept together in the same aviary.

Requirements in captivity: Yellow-rumped Finches are not suited for cage life, but they can be integrated into a mixed group of exotic finches because they never behave aggressively. Being in a group not only agrees with their sociable nature but also gives them a chance to pick their own mates. But if several pairs of these birds are kept in adjacent aviaries, their social needs are sometimes so great that they try

A Yellow-rumped Finch is shown on the left.

to join the birds in the other aviary and pay no attention to their own partners.

One corner of the aviary should always be planted with tall grass and reeds, and the temperature in the aviary should be at least 65°F (18°C).

Food: Small- and large-grained millet, sprouted spike millet, and other sprouted seeds such as oats; mealworms, ant pupae.

Breeding: Since these birds are extremely choosy about their partners, the best results are achieved if the pairs can form freely. Birds that are already building nests encourage the nesting instinct in others. These finches usually nest in semiopen nesting boxes and sometimes in thick bushes. Fresh and dry grass serves as building material. A clutch consists of three to five eggs, and both parents are reliable brooders.

For raising their young, Yellow-rumped Finches need more animal protein than other closely related species. They should therefore get mealworms, ant pupae, and egg food in addition to green grass seeds and greens. The parents continue feeding the young birds for another three to five weeks after the fledglings learn how to fly.

Chestnut-breasted Finch
Lonchura casthaneothorax

Description: 4¼ inches (11 cm).

Male: Crown, back of head, and nape, gray-brown with a dark stripe across the middle of the feathers; back, cinnamon brown; wings, rump, and tail, gray-brown; central tail feathers, yellow; sides of head and throat, black; crop and upper breast, chestnut brown and set off from the white lower belly by a black band.

Female: Colors muted; there is no mark to tell her from the male.

Distribution and habitat: Wet lowlands; swamps, rice, sugarcane, and grain fields in northern and eastern Australia and as far south as Sydney; New Guinea.

This species has expanded its range, moving into areas with artificial irrigation.

Habits: Chestnut-breasted Finches live in gregarious communities all year-round. They live on green barley and rice and on the seeds of other cultivated and wild grasses, picking them directly from the standing stalk.

In the second half of the rainy season—and, in irrigated areas, early in the dry season, too—pairs build their nests between the vertical stems of tall grass or reeds. Long blades of grass are piled up into a firm bed for the five to six eggs and the hollow is padded with soft grass inflorescences. The young are fed insects.

Requirements in captivity: Chestnut-breasted Finches are usually fairly long-lived in captivity, but they should not live in a cage all the time because they tend to get fat. In an aviary, however, they are quite vivacious and display a highly developed social activity. They get along harmoniously with each other and with other species and defend their immediate nesting area only during mating season. A further reason for keeping these birds in groups is that they prompt each other to build nests. Since they clamber around most of the time in grass and reeds and nest there, one corner of the aviary should offer thick vegetation of this kind.

Chestnut-breasted Finches do not sleep in their nests and need a minimum temperature of 65°F (18°C).

Food: Small- and large-grained millet, sprouted spike millet, lots of chickweed, green grass seed, mealworms, ant pupae.

Breeding: In a properly designed aviary Chestnut-breasted Finches usually breed readily. They are not fussy about nesting sites; some build in thick bushes, others accept nesting boxes, but all sites must be well concealed so that the pairs do not distract each other. In addition to the usual building materials, Chestnut-breasted Finches have a preference for long, green blades of grass, and they need fine, dry grass for padding.

The young hatch after 13 days and grow up without problems if there are enough mealworms, ant pupae, and greens available. After learning how to fly at three weeks of age, they still return to the nest for a few nights for sleeping.

Young Chestnut-breasted Finches, too, mature quite early but should not be allowed to breed until they are 9 to 12 months old.

Pictorella Finch
Lonchura pectoralis

Description: 4¾ inches (12 cm).

Male: Crown, nape, and upper side, brownish silver gray with white spots on the wings; sides of head, lores, and throat, black and bordered by a narrow reddish band; tail, blackish brown; upper breast, white (the feathers have a black crossband near the tip but the black is visible only on the sides); belly, gray with reddish cast.

Female: Black areas on head smaller and more brownish black; the black on the white breast feathers more visible.

Distribution and habitat: Extended grassy areas without taller vegetation, dry steppes with scattered low bushes, and semiarid regions in northern Australia from Derby to eastern Queensland.

Habits: Except during mating season, Pictorella Finches live in small groups. They pick their food—green and mature seeds of grasses—off the ground or out of seed heads on the ground as well as out of the standing grass.

In the second half of the rainy season the pairs build nests in low bushes or tufts of grass. Grass stalks, roots, and small twigs are used for building. The hollow of the nest is padded with fine grasses and a few feathers. The four to six young are raised on insects, primarily termites that are caught on the wing.

Requirements in captivity: If kept exclusively in a cage, these birds always stay timorous and nervous, but in an aviary they lose their shyness. Since they defend only the immediate vicinity of their nests during the breeding season and are otherwise perfectly peaceful, they are well suited for a mixed community. But they should have thick bushes, tufts of grass, and branches of broom at various heights for nesting, as well as a fairly large open area covered with sand for their courtship display.

Like all other Australian finches, the Pictorella Finch needs temperatures of at least 65°F (18°C), which means that an outdoor aviary has to be connected to a warm room where the birds can stay in cooler weather.

Food: Millet, spike millet, lots of chickweed, green seeds, mealworms, waxmoth larvae, ant pupae.

Breeding: Pairs of Pictorella Finches are not as closely attached to each other as Long-tailed Grass-finches, but they can be bred quite successfully in captivity. Some pairs build their nests underneath thick

Java Sparrows can often be found in large flocks.

bushes or in the grass directly on the ground; others like to locate them in an aviary corner hidden in ivy or broom; but they also accept semiopen nesting boxes. Coconut and aloe fibers, fresh grass, small twigs, and pine needles are accepted as building materials, and grass stalks are used to reinforce the walls of the nest. Both partners are good sitters, and the young hatch after 14 days. If there are enough mealworms, ant pupae, and waxmoth larvae available, the parents raise the nestlings without complications. The young birds leave the nest after three weeks.

Java Sparrow
Padda oryzivora

Description: 5½ inches (14 cm).

Male and female: Head, rump, tail, and wings, black; back and wing coverts, soft bluish gray; sides of head, white; chin and a narrow band running to the back of the neck, black; throat and breast, bluish gray; belly, light pinkish gray.

There are also white and off-white variants of the Java Sparrow.

Distribution and habitat: Occurred originally only on Java and Bali in village gardens, plantations, and woods as well as in wild grasslands with scattered areas of woods and brush; has now been introduced into many tropical countries.

Habits: Outside of the mating season, Java Sparrows often stay together in large flocks. They live on various grass seeds and at harvest time almost exclusively on maturing rice kernels that they pick out of the seed heads.

After the rainy season they build their nests under roofs, on beams, in thornbushes, in hollow trees or climbing vines. The nests are loosely built of grass stalks. The female lays four to seven eggs, and the young are raised primarily on green seeds.

Requirements in captivity: Java Sparrows are not very particular about their food or their quarters. Because of the size of this bird, a cage must be at least 4 feet (1.2 m) long. During the mating period the birds—at least the originally wild gray Java Sparrow—should be kept in an aviary with plenty of open space because they fly around vigorously. Java Sparrows are absolutely trustworthy in a mixed community, even though smaller species are sometimes intimidated by their sheer size.

Food: Canary, small- and large-grained and spike millet, rice, barley, oats, sprouted millet, green seeds, chickweed, egg food, ant pupae, mealworms.

Breeding: Breeding the white variant of the Java Sparrow presents no problems, but breeding the originally wild form is more difficult and often ends in failure. The difficulties can often be overcome by offering a large variety of foods and keeping a group of birds together because they stimulate each other's instinct for nest building. Java Sparrows seldom choose natural nesting sites but prefer parakeet nesting boxes that are wider than they are high. They will also accept regular enclosed or semiopen boxes. The nest is built of coconut fibers, dry grass stalks, moss, bast, and pieces of yarn. The dark-colored young hatch after 13 to 14 days. Then the parent birds need plenty of egg food, ant pupae, and mealworms in order to raise their offspring, which leave the nest after three to four weeks.

Cutthroat
Amadina fasciata

Description: 4¾ to 5¼ inches (12–13.5 cm).

Male: Upper side, gray-brown with black crossbarring; back, with blackish crossbands; inner secondaries, with light rims on tips and on the distal faces before the secondaries, a wide black crossband; tail, black-brown; throat and cheeks, white with a blood red ribbon across the lower throat to the auricular regions; belly, off-white with blackish striations; chestnut brown spot on middle of belly.

Female: Without the red ribbon at the throat or the spot on the belly; dark striations on sides of head.

Distribution and habitat: Dry savannas and thornbush scrub south of the Sahara from western Africa to the Red Sea; in eastern Africa south as far as Tanzania; Rhodesia, Botswana, and Transvaal.

Habits: Cutthroats live in large flocks outside of the mating season but are always in pairs to breed. They find their food—mostly grass seeds, but also termites—on the ground.

They build their nests at the end of the rainy season in bushes, trees, or hollows in trees. The nests are built of grass stalks and lined with feathers. Cutthroats will also take over abandoned weavers' nests, which they also like to use as sleeping nests. A clutch consists of four to five eggs, and the young are raised primarily on ripening seeds.

Requirements in captivity: Cutthroats make few demands, are very animated, and not nervous. But at the beginning they require temperatures around 77°F (25°C). Most of them are peaceful, but during the mating season, some individuals may develop into bullies that attack and mercilessly chase other kinds of exotic finches or drive pairs of other species from their nests. The keeper therefore has to be on a constant watch. If kept exclusively in cages,

Cutthroats tend to lethargy; they should therefore be kept in a spacious, densely planted aviary when not breeding, especially since group living stimulates their mating instinct.

Food: Mixed millet, spike millet, sprouted and green seeds, egg food, ant pupae, mealworms, pieces of oranges, pears, and apples.

Breeding: Unfortunately, Cutthroats do not breed well in captivity. They abandon eggs or even nestlings for no apparent reason. It is essential to offer them as many different kinds of nesting sites as possible (semiopen and closed nesting boxes, various kinds of old nests), coarse building materials (hay, bast, stems of millet, shredded paper), and feathers for the inside of the nest.

The Cutthroat is a good choice for the nonexpert bird owner.

Female Cutthroats are often afflicted with egg binding and should be given food enriched with vitamins and codliver oil. Refrain from nest checks because the birds are easily disturbed. Since individual pairs have different preferences, the rearing foods should be as varied as possible to let the birds choose what they like.

Another member of the genus *Amadina* is the Red-headed Finch *(A. erythrocephala)*, 5 inches (13 cm), which, apart from the red head (dull gray-brown in the female), is grayish black on the top and brown below. The brown belly is dotted with white spots rimmed in black. Red-headed Finches inhabit the almost desertlike sand steppes near water in the Kalahari and tree and thornbush steppes in South Africa and Botswana. They feed primarily on ripe and—when available—ripening seeds. These birds raise their young mostly in empty nests of sparrows and weavers or in the communal nests of some weavers. This somewhat heavier species is less suitable for cage life. Its requirements for food and breeding are similar to those for Cutthroats, but Red-headed Finches seem to be somewhat better breeders.

Chapter Nine
Aviary Communities

This table shows which birds can be kept in pairs only and which can live in groups. It also indicates which species do not get along with each other. Purple Grenadiers, for instance, have to be kept in separate pairs and cannot be combined with Cordon-bleus. But aggressive behavior occurs even in species with a reputation for being peaceful, and it is therefore important that you watch your birds regularly. This will allow you to intervene in time and prevent disasters.

Explanation of Symbols

○ To be kept in separate pairs; not to be combined with other species.

∝ To be kept in pairs all year-round; can be combined with other species.

◇ To be kept in separate pairs during mating season, otherwise, in groups; can be combined with other species.

● Several males and females can be kept together in a group together with other species.

✕ Cannot be combined with other species.

A striking finch rests on a leaf.

Species	Cutthroat and Red-headed Finch	Mannikins of the genus *Lochura* (subgenus *Spermestes*)	Gray-headed Munia	Silverbills	Spice Finch	White-backed Munia	Finches of the genus *Lochura*, munias, and Pictorella, Chestnut-breasted, and Yellow-rumped Finches	Java Sparrow	Parrot Finches and Gouldian Finch	Masked Grassfinch	Parson Finch	Long-tailed Grassfinch	Zebra Finch	Bicheno Finch
Melba Finch														
Orange-winged Pytilia														
other Pytilias														
Dybowski's Twinspot														
Green Twinspot														
Peter's Twinspot														
Brown and Bar-breasted Firefinches														
Jameson's Firefinch														
Black-bellied Firefinch														
other firefinches of the genus *Lagonosticta*														
Cordon-bleus														
Purple Grenadier														
Violet-eared Waxbill														
Lavender Waxbill														
Black-cheeked Waxbill														
Orange-cheeked Waxbill														
other waxbills of the genus *Estrilda*														
Swee Waxbill														
Quail Finch														
Avadavat														
Green Avadavat														
Goldbreast														
Diamond Firetail														
Painted Finch														
Crimson Finch														
Star Finch														
Cherry Finch														
Bicheno Finch														●
Zebra Finch													●	
Long-tailed Grassfinch												∝		
Parson Finch											○	X		
Masked Grassfinch										●		X		
Parrot Finches and Gouldian Finch									●					
Java Sparrow								●						
Finches of the genus *Lonchura*, munias, and Pictorella, Chestnut-breasted, and Yellow-rumped Finches							●							
White-backed Munia						◇								
Spice Finch					●									
Silverbills				●										
Gray-headed Munia			●											
Mannikins of the genus *Lonchura* (subgenus *Spermestes*)		◇												
Cutthroat and Red-headed Finch	○													

Melba Finch	∝			×		×																																					
Orange-winged Pytilia	×	∝		×		×																																					
other Pytilias	×		●	×		×																																					
Dybowski's Twinspot				∝																																							
Green Twinspot					●																																						
Peter's Twinspot						∝																																					
Brown and Bar-breasted Firefinches						×	○		×																																		
Jameson's Firefinch						×		∝	×																																		
Black-bellied Firefinch						×			∝																																		
other firefinches of the genus *Lagonosticta*						×			×	●																																	
Cordon-bleus											◇	×																															
Purple Grenadier												×	∝																														
Violet-eared Waxbill													×	◇																													
Lavender Waxbill															●																												
Black-cheeked Waxbill																◇																											
Orange-cheeked Waxbill																	●																										
other waxbills of the genus *Estrilda*																		●																									
Swee Waxbill																			●																								
Quail Finch																				◇																							
Avadavat																					◇																						
Green Avadavat																						◇																					
Goldbreast																																											
Diamond Firetail																							○																				
Painted Finch																								●																			
Crimson Finch																									○																		
Star Finch	×			×																						●																	
Cherry Finch																																											

Useful Addresses and Literature

Associations

American Friends of Aviculture
P.O. Box 1568
Redondo Beach, CA 90278

Association of Avian Veterinarians
P.O. Box 299
East Northport, NY 11731

Avicultural Society of America, Inc.
8228 Sulphur Road
Ojai, CA 93023

Avicultural Advancement Council
P.O. Box 5126
Postal Station B
Victoria, BC V4C 3H6
Canada

Avicultural Society of Australia
Box 130
Broadford, Victoria 3658
Australia

National Finch and Softbill Society
P.O. Box 3232
Ballwin, MO 63022

Periodicals

Australian Birdkeeper
P.O. Box 6288
South Tweeds Heads
New South Wales 2468
Australia

Avicultural Bulletin
P.O. Box 2796
Redondo Beach, CA 90278

Avicultural Magazine
The Avicultural Society
Windsor, Forest Stud, Mill Ride
Ascot, Berkshire, England

Bird Talk
P.O. Box 6050
Mission Viejo, CA 92690

Watchbird
American Federation of Aviculture
P.O. Box 1568
Redondo Beach, CA 90278

Books

Alderton, David A. *A Birdkeeper's Guide to Finches.* Blackburgs, VA: Tetra Press, 1988.

Burgmann, Petra. *Feeding Your Pet Bird.* Hauppauge, NY: Barron's Educational Series, Inc., 1993.

Mobbs, A. J. *The Complete Book of Australian Finches.* London: Merehurst Ltd., 1990.

Vriends, Matthew. *Gouldian Finches.* Hauppauge, NY: Barron's Educational Series, Inc., 1991.

____. *Hand-feeding and Raising Baby Birds.* Hauppauge, NY: Barron's Educational Series, Inc., 1996.

____. Simon & Schuster's *Guide to Pet Birds.* New York: Simon & Schuster, 1995.

____. *The New Bird Handbook.* Hauppauge, NY: Barron's Educational Series, Inc., 1989.

These finches eye their surroundings from the safety of tree branches.

Index